REALMS

Copyright © 2015 by Brad Huebert

Previously released as "Finding Home: A Parable of Kingdom Life" in 2009

All rights reserved. No part of this book may be used or reproduced by any means, graphic, electronic, or mechanical, including photocopying, recording, taping or by any information storage retrieval system without the written permission of the author except in the case of brief quotations embodied in critical articles and reviews.

This is a work of fiction. All of the characters, names, incidents, organizations, and dialogue in this novel are either the products of the author's imagination or are used fictitiously.

Also by Brad Huebert:

Beloved: Some Fairy Tales Are True

Go With The Flow: A Non-Religious Approach To Your Daily Time With God

Acknowledgments

Shauna—you are my warrior princess, my greatest fan, my wife for life, my best friend, my partner in ministry. Noah, Glory, and Joel, my rockin' kids who aren't kids anymore—you bring such joy to my heart and I'm proud of you. And finally my King— the magnificent God of awesome, my one and only Saviour, Jesus Christ—you breathe life into me every single day and I love you so much it hurts. I trust you. You're everything to me. Thanks for letting me do this.

INTR⊕DUCTI⊕N

Bone-headed dude that I am, I arm-wrestled this stupid manuscript for eight years before figuring out why I couldn't pin it to the table.

It's a book about the kingdom of God.

When Jesus taught about his kingdom, he chucked traditional outlines. He never hammered out a blog series or punched out a three-point sermon. When it came to teaching the kingdom, Jesus' methods were simple: He either demonstrated his power— actually doing what he wanted people to see—or he captured their imaginations with stories that got under their skin. Good stories do that, don't they? They eat at you, poke you, slip through the back door of your soul and join you for breakfast.

After kicking myself—repeatedly—which would probably have made a great YouTube video—I scrapped eight years of work and started over. The story wrote itself in about two weeks.

The original version of this story was entitled "Finding Home: A Parable of Kingdom Life." It went on to publication in Germany, where it's currently in its fourth printing. It's been fun to dive back into the story and refresh it for you.

There's something you should know about the main character. He's not some iconic superhero you could never relate to. He's actually me, a regular guy like you. Most of the revelations 'he' experiences throughout the story were lifted from real moments of struggles and fist-bumping in my own journey. I think my life is a lot like yours, which means this story can describe your story, too.

My advice? Read *Realms* more than once. There's a lot to chew on. The truths embedded in the story are gospel truths, which means they can and will change your life if you let them. I can hardly wait to hear your part of the story!

One last thing: Since I'm the one writing this thing, I'm going to take the liberty of indulging myself on one minor point: messing with my name and my family to make the story work for print. I heard once that people who view their life through an 'epic story' lens tend to find it more fulfilling. I totally agree, so that's where I—I mean, Clint—is going to take you.

The best thing about telling the truth with a story is that I can actually show you what I think Jesus means and gives and does without pages and pages of footnotes. I can unveil the world as it might look if you could press through the clammy threshold of flesh to see with the eyes of faith. And maybe, just maybe, as we do that together, our eyes really will be opened and nothing will ever be the same for either of us.

Wouldn't that be amazing?

CHAPTER ⊕NE
BASILEIA

In the three hours since Monica backed the silver Highlander out of the driveway, Clint had watched two and a half mindless episodes on Netflix, wiped down the kitchen counter, eaten a really bad orange, mowed the back lawn, read four paragraphs of an article about migrating seals, opened the fridge to sniff the leftovers, and almost knelt down to hand over his life to Jesus at least a dozen times. He'd been what most people call a Christian for a long time, but the thought of giving total control to God just about gave him hives. Or worse.

He glanced at the clock. Sixty-eight hours left of the weekend. Monica and Sarah had bombed down the coast to Mom and Dad's to give him space to think, to get right with God. It seemed like a good idea at the time. Now they were gone, he missed them like crazy, and he'd used up every distraction to pass the time he could think of. Going solo was probably a good thing, but the house was a whole lot warmer with his girls in it.

He picked up a framed photo of the three of them taken at the beach last summer. And smiled wistfully. They were all standing by the weathered blue dock, arm in arm—but Monica and Sarah had something he didn't. Funny, even his iPhone camera caught it. And that 'something' was clear as day. Their warmth. Their sparkle. Their life.

He wanted it too—that simple faith, that joy, or whatever it was—which meant he needed to hunker down, pray, and be done with it. No more excuses.

Excuses? Is that what his resistance was made of? Probably.

But excuses were lame, so it was time. Sliding off the couch, he dropped to his knees on the living room carpet, eyes clenched shut. No hives yet. He was determined not to move until the deed was done.

A giant sigh shuddered through him, bubbling up like wine popping a stubborn cork.

"Okay, okay. I give up, Jesus. You know I believe in you, right? In your death for me, your resurrection, the whole deal. And so I guess the answer is yes. This is it. I'm all yours. Your move."

As he spoke, the swirling fragments of his fuzzy faith found each other and took shape. Something shifted inside him. Died. Laughed. Jumped to life. All at once.

His heart now belonged to God, he could feel it. Feel *him*. And new life. Which meant he and his girls now shared another special bond. He had to call them.

Clint opened his eyes, then scanned for the phone. But the light around him had changed. And the air. A breeze was swirling its way past him. A breeze? Yup. A breeze, slipping through living room windows that no longer existed.

He gasped.

He was kneeling on a magnificent stone bridge—white as snow lit by the sun. The bridge stretched more than a mile, spanning a chasm so deep he couldn't bring himself to look all the way down because it made him woozy. He was parked in the middle, right at the crest of the structure's slow arc. A cold rectangular spire punctured the sky above him, and directly ahead the bridge sloped gently downward, eventually kissing a wall encircling a city sparkling on the mountain.

A bead of sweat snaked through his hairline, biting his eyes. But he didn't blink. Not a chance. He didn't want to miss a thing. Where on earth was he?

Standing up carefully, Clint turned around. He saw another city at the other end of the bridge. This one was inky black, dressed head-to-toe in toxic plumes of smoke. Hundreds and even thousands of winged creatures circled like vultures above it. The sight made his blood thicken in his veins.

The bridge was solid but Clint took tentative steps toward the bright city. The gentle breeze he'd felt earlier held the place in an empty, even eerie silence, making the bridge feel not so much like a place as a place between places. The only real sounds came from his shuffling feet and now and then, his tongue smacking his lips.

Clint finally allowed himself to blink. Twice. Nothing changed. "Okay, so this is officially bizarre."

As he drew nearer to the 'nice' city, Clint thought it looked kind of like a wedding cake baked onto a gold mountain. A thousand candy-green banners waved gently from the wall's ramparts and its towers were frosted by beautiful clouds. Kinda. And a huge tree sat just to the right of the road, right outside what looked like what would be a front gate.

He also noticed with some relief that the gate was wide open. It looked friendly enough. Again he wondered: Where was he? Candyland?

As he neared the gate, hearty singing greeted him. The closer he came to the giant doorway, the louder the song became. That, and the city grew brighter. Was he dead? Was this the door into heaven? His heart leapt at the thought until he read the giant letters engraved above the gates:

Basileia.

Before he could ponder the name, people were streaming out of the gateway and cavorting toward him. Yeah, cavorting. Their faces were beaming as they danced. Turning to look behind him to see who or what they were so excited to see, he saw nothing.

He whirled back around to meet a bent-over woman with a brown shawl. A dozen others with shining eyes and genuine smiles approached and then encircled him, hugging him and patting him on the back like he was some kind of war hero.

"You've come, you've come."

"Hey, cool. I guess so. But where am I, exactly?"

The woman raised her left eyebrow. "Basileia, of course. You gave your heart to the King."

"Sure, okay," Clint replied, remembering his prayer. "But that happened in another place. Not here. How could you—"

"Another place, yes," a little boy said, nodding in agreement. "From back there. From Kakos." He was pointing toward the black city. Clint smiled at the boy, trying to help him understand.

"No, not from… uh… Kakos. I've never been there before."

"Yes you have. We all have. We all come from the black city. We all come from Kakos."

Clint was about to correct the child when the whole group said in unison, "Kakos is our mother, but Basileia is our home."

8

"Wow, okay. Am I dead? Or is somebody wearing a GoPro or something?"

"No, not dead," said the woman. "Alive, fully alive!"

"So then this is heaven?" Clint was growing impatient.

"We already told you," the first boy said, grinning. "It's Basileia. That means 'kingdom.'"

"Kingd… but where is my family? My house? My Highlander? It's an SUV, pretty good on gas…"
The group laughed again, patting him on the back.

"We're your family now. Welcome here." With that, the whole crew turned around and cavorted their way back through the gate. Clint blinked slowly, still confused beyond reason.

Basileia? The kingdom? But not heaven? He didn't recognize any church friends in the group, and he was pretty sure he'd met most Monica's relatives, all except the ones from the Australian outback. So who were these people? It was all too weird.

Put off by the dancing greeters, he glanced back at the black city again and shuddered. Darkness or dancers? He couldn't remember ever seeing Kakos before, but it did feel vaguely familiar. That said, he decided to take his chances inside Basileia. He marched himself right through the giant gate.

Standing just inside, Clint paused to get his bearings. A few paces ahead stood a proud golden wall. To his left an archway opened into something or other, and to his right, an ascending stone staircase curled out of sight.

"Old City or New City?" asked a drawling voice to his left. He turned to see a portly man lobbing grins at him from his seat behind a merchant's cart. He was missing a few teeth and his tangled red hair flopped over his eyebrows. Clint smiled in return.

"Hey. I'm new to Basla."

"Ba-sillay-uh," the man said slowly, cocking his head.

"Ok. Sure. Basilyuhaya. Uh."

"No, that's not it." The man's eyes popped wide suddenly. "Oh, but I'm sorry. Ya don't even have yer book yet, do ya? I forgot."

"My book?"

"I'm supposed'ta give new people their book. That's my job." He grinned dumbly, holding out a thick leather-bound volume. "Here. Don't lose it, ok? They're kind of magic and they're expensive and stuff."

Clint took it and began flipping through the endless pages. "Thanks, I think. What's it for?"

"It tells ya how."

"How what?"

"Old City or New City?"

Clint sighed, deciding he would get nowhere with the old cod. "I have no idea. Old, new... which do most people choose?"

"The Old City, most always." The man's face was expressionless. Like a really bad poker face.

"Old City it is, then." Clint strode toward the staircase.

"Like I said, it tells ya how." The man was trying to be helpful, but Clint felt like he was being barked at by a simpleton.

"Right, I got that, but—"

"How ta be a good citizen. Of the Old City."

"Hey, that's super. Thanks." Clint tucked the book under his arm, waving over his shoulder as he bounded up the steps. Time to figure out where he was.

Emerging on a cobblestoned second level, Clint scanned his surroundings. He'd found an ancient suburb or neighbourhood or something. The city was slightly smaller there because it sat a little higher on the mountain than the main level. Dozens of townspeople were milling around him, minding their own business as they bustled through their tasks for the day. The dancers were on break, apparently. A bit farther down the street some kind of market sprawled through the street like it owned the place.

At the urging of his complaining stomach, he decided to explore in that direction first. After a bite to eat, he would ask for directions. He wondered if they took debit.

The market was quaint, but it was fully stocked. Kind of like a life-sized Dickens Village complete with fresh produce, fish, strung chickens, and piles of colourful nuts.

"New to Basileia?"

Clint turned to face one of the merchants, a middle-aged woman standing behind a pyramid of bright green apples.

"Yeah. I flew in just a few minutes ago."

"Flew in?"

"Yeah. Flight One-oh-weird."

"I don't…"

"It's a joke. I kinda just appeared on the bridge out there. Poof. Teleported or whatever. The dancers saw me in."

"Well then, welcome home."

"Home?"

"Home. Here, try one." She tossed him an apple.

"Oh, I don't have any money. I left my wallet on the island."

"The island?"

"Beside the fridge."

She blinked at him like he was speaking another language.

"Re-fridge-er-a-tor."

"You seem hungry," she replied, smiling politely. "Keep it."

"You're a good person. Truly."

Clint bit hard into the fruit—partly because he was hungry and partly because he thought the apple might snap him back to his leather couch in the living room. It was a really good apple, but unfortunately this reality didn't budge. He was about to wander away to explore more of the city when he paused, rocking on his heels a moment.

"Something on your mind?" She raised a curious eyebrow.

"Everything, mostly. But I've got this nagging sense that I ought to be doing something in particular."

"Sure you do. We all have that. Some people think that once you arrive here the feeling will pass, but that's not true. It's usually a gentle pressure, kind of a weight put there by the King. If you're especially faithful the feeling actually grows. It's quite normal."

"Normal, huh? I'll take your word for it, but what should I do about the feeling for now?"

"Have you read your book yet? The book will tell you everything."

He patted the book cover. "Just got it. And to tell you the truth, I don't plan on staying. I need to get home. But this'll make a killer souvenir."

"Well, if you read the book every day from now on, it will tell you what to do and answer your questions. See?" She pointed to the cover. Words had been sewn into the bleached leather, words Clint was pretty sure hadn't been there when toothless Joe held it out to him. *The Book of Duties*, apparently.

"Okay, so it's like a Bible. Where do I start?"

The woman wiggled her way around the cart and strode over to him. Taking the book, she paged through it until she found a place near the beginning. She slipped a strip of brown paper between the pages and thumped the book closed.

"There." She smiled as she returned the volume. "Start slow," she said. "There's a lot to learn, and it can get pretty complicated later on. Just be sure not to miss Temple on Tuesday."

"Temple?"

"All faithful citizens meet at the temple once a week to worship the King. The ceremony starts at eight in the evening."

"The King? You mean Jesus?"

"Here we just call him the King."

"Works for me. Thanks for the apple and the advice. I guess I'll see you on Tuesday, if I haven't figured things out by then."

As he said the words, he noticed a little park further up the street with a free bench in the shade. He decided to sit there for a while to read his new book. Maybe there was a section called, 'How to click your heels together and go home.' If he was lucky, it would have a glossary at the back to help him understand all the new words he was hearing. Kakos. Basileia. Duty. Temple.

Temple. He called out to the woman again. "One last question. What day is it today?"

"Monday."

"And that temple thing ..."

"On Tuesday. Tomorrow. Eight o'clock."

"Right."

Chapter Two
The Book of Duties

Clint did find a glossary near the back of the Book of Duties. Unfortunately, there were no maps. Or comics. Or magic prayers.

Flipping through the pages, he soon discovered the kid on the bridge was right: Basileia did mean "kingdom." He also learned Kakos meant "evil." Which made sense. He'd left his old life of failure and sin behind. He'd surrendered his whole heart to Jesus—or rather, the King. Apparently that meant living here in Basileia. Funny, his pastor had never mentioned that. Where was his pastor?

Even more important, where was Basileia? And how did he get here? He searched the index up and down, tracing it with his finger. Not a single entry that might explain how he got from his living room to this strange medieval kingdom. Truth be told, he might have thought twice about praying the prayer if he'd known what he was getting himself into. After all, what about his family? His friends back home? His job? His new Highlander? Had he left all those things behind forever?

Clint shook his head. The King had changed everything he knew, everything he cared about. He had to get home as soon as possible. Maybe this was all a dream or some kind of bizarre vision. A virtual reality game room, like Oculus Rift 2.0 for radical Christians.

Finding the brown paper bookmark given to him by the merchant woman, he prayed again. "Lord—I mean, King, or whoever—I'm not sure what's going on. I'm totally clueless here. I hope this book of yours helps me get back home." He wondered if he would actually get to meet the King in person before leaving.

Clint began reading. It didn't take long to see that the King had stacked a good chunk of the book with to-do lists. It was like his church back home, then. Being a free spirit, Clint wasn't much of a list person, but if he was supposed to use the lists to please the King, he could make it work for awhile.

He felt like a clueless child learning how to live all over again —how to walk, how to talk, how to eat, how to do business, how to pray, how to worship. Clint felt a wave of panic until he recalled the shrewd words of the merchant. "Take it slow. There is much to learn."

"I'll say." Clint decided to choose one section for the time being and focus on putting it into practice. After nailing down one issue, he could move on to another one. Scanning the list of lists in the back of the book, he found something that said, "Devotional Correctness." He wasn't sure what "devotional" meant but he did know he wanted to be correct, so he flipped to page 381 and began to read.

"Good citizens of Basileia are devotionally correct citizens. Every good citizen must spend time every day reading the Book of Duties and praying to the King. It's what he expects of us. No exceptions."

It made sense, really. He'd given himself to the King. So no more fence-sitting. He would reserve the King a block of time every morning. That way once he found the guy, he'd have a few brownie points stacked up in his favour. If the King was happy with him, maybe he would teleport him back into his living room or unplug him from the Matrix. Although, if it really was like the Matrix, he would have to try running up walls and dodging bullets before he left. Maybe there was a Morpheus in town who could help him learn Kung Fu.

Reading on, Clint found a following section very helpful. It outlined how much time to spend in his devotions, what to say and do during the time, and how to make sure the King liked it. It was all so complicated, but he had a mission now.

His heart pounded when he realized that at that very instant he was doing what the King had commanded him to do. Not only that, the birds were singing around him and the sun even felt warm on his skin. It was like Alice in Wonderland. No wonder people had been singing at the gate. Maybe he'd join them tomorrow. No, not tomorrow. He'd be gone by then, Lord willing. And he didn't know any of the songs. Ignorance was bliss.

Looking up from his reading, he got another surprise. Planted just across the cobbled street from the park sat a row of quaintly dressed houses. In the middle of the row was a newer looking unit, freshly painted, with a thick woven banner stretched across the front door. "Welcome home, Clint," it read.

"You've got to be…" It had to be a mistake. Clint leapt to his feet, almost forgetting his book on the bench. After making a bee-line across the street, he bounced up the two steps to the door and ripped the welcome off the opening. He grabbed the door handle, opening it with a creak.

"Hello?" His voice reverberated through the home, but no one else named Clint answered. As he stepped into the entrance, he scanned the dwelling. It was simple but clean and attractive. A fresh cot had been made up in the corner, a fire was already busy in the stove, and a whimsically crooked window faced the outer wall of the city.

He immediately noticed the opening gave him a great view of the bridge, the chasm, and Kakos beyond it. Kakos. His mind reviewed all the things he'd learned in Sunday School growing up. Perhaps figuratively speaking he had come from the evil city, as the boy had insisted. And yet, Basileia wasn't figurative.

Just then Clint spotted a crystal goblet on the kitchen table. A small note-card had been placed next to it. It was a personal message from the King!

Clint, have a drink on me. I hope to see you in the New City soon.

~ The King

Clint's heart thumped. A personal note from the King. Which meant he really could meet the King and find his way home. On the other hand, it would be fun to visit Basileia with his family once the confusion had been sorted out. As tourists, mind you. It was a fun place to visit, but not the greatest place to live.

The note gave Clint a surge of energy. He sat at the table, savouring the freshly poured water in the goblet. He opened the book to where he'd left off, poring over list after list after list, making notes and praying for the King's favour in hopes that he'd be able to keep all the commandments so he could learn to please him.

The truth seemed overwhelming. Tipping the cup for another sip, he noticed the water was gone. Too bad. It was the most refreshing water he'd ever tasted.

Pushing his chair back from the table, he decided to take a walk to pass the time and clear his head. The stroll through the park did him good, though he felt strangely weary in the late afternoon light. He noticed that the sun didn't seem as bright as it had when he arrived. Oddly enough, the buildings didn't seem so radiant either. He shook his head. He was probably imagining it. After all, it had been a long, momentous day. Maybe he'd wake up at home in the real world the next morning. It was entirely possible that this whole adventure would turn out to be a vivid dream. Maybe his pastor could interpret it for him after church next week. Or recommend a good shrink. Or a stiff drink.

As he walked, he tried to remember what he'd learned in the Book of Duties. Every so often he saw something happening around him that reminded him of an entry on a list he had studied—a child in need, a woman requiring help. Most of the time he snapped into action, happily doing what the King expected of him in the situations that arose. It was like following the Bible.

But there was no end to it all. The needs were everywhere, and there was a command for everyone and everything. Sometimes two or three somethings sprung up at once and Clint didn't know which command to obey. A few times he just froze, doing nothing.

Frustration started to gum up in his heart. And then discouragement. He was too new at this. He wasn't Basileian enough yet. There was no way to obey every command on the giant list. No way.

Before long, he decided that enough was enough and called it a day. The sun was going down by then, so it seemed like the right thing to do—unless of course there was a rule against flagrant sulking.

Arriving at the house assigned to him exhausted and depressed, Clint knelt beside his bed and muttered a long tearful prayer into the bedding, telling the King how sorry he was for not keeping the list faithfully while secretly hoping he hadn't blown his opportunity to go home. He resolved to get up early the next morning to read more of the lists so he would stand a better chance at keeping them during the day.

Somewhere in the middle of his prayer, still sprawled over the bed-frame, Clint fell into a patchy sleep. He dreamt of Kakos, but strangely enough, it didn't seem like a nightmare. It felt like relief. He didn't care.

Clint awoke the next morning to a deranged rooster crowing not far from his window. The creature's call vibrated up and down his spine like an electric shock.

"I'm up, I'm up!" Clint leapt from the bed, reacting like he had to report to the insipid bird. After stretching out some stiffness, his heart sank. He was still in Basileia. A moment later he remembered his promise to get up early to study and pray. Clint rolled back onto his knees. They were tender from all the praying he had done the day before. He was just about to bow his head when he heard a knock at the door.

"What now?" Clint stomped over to the door to answer. He swung it open and found the merchant woman standing on his porch. She cradled a basket of fresh green apples.

"Good morning." Her usual smile eclipsed her face again.

"Hello."

"Is this a bad time? I brought you more apples."

Clint glanced back at the bed and his unopened Book of Duties. His eyes dropped to the floor. "No, it's fine. Come in."

"I see you're still here. How did you fare yesterday? Did you read the book?"

Clint ushered her inside, then sat at the table as she set the basket on it.

He rubbed his eyes. "Some of it. Enough to keep me busy until bedtime yesterday."

Her eyes sparkled. "That's wonderful!"

"Wonderful? I totally sucked at it, and I'm exhausted."

"Well, it was your first day, after all."

"I guess." Clint shifted in his seat.

"You're young in the faith, Clint. You'll catch on." She did look convinced of that point, which was something.

But Clint didn't want to catch on. He wanted to go home. To have his life back. "What about you? You seem to have it going on. Do you keep the list perfectly?"

The woman paused, then bent in close, lowering her voice. She looked around pensively, as if to make sure no one was eavesdropping. "We don't really talk about this, but the truth is, no one keeps the lists perfectly."

"No one? That's a relief."

"That's right. But you eventually learn a few tricks to get around it."

"Tricks?"

"Well, not tricks, exactly. Call it a choice of emphasis. Did you notice some things on the lists are more public and obvious, while others are more inward and hidden?"

"Sure, I guess so, but aren't ..."

She didn't let him finish. "Focus on the public ones, Clint. The ones people see. When they see you keep the 'big' things in order they'll assume you're keeping the other rules, the ones they can't see."

Clint was confused. "If you're all faking it, don't you know that beneath the surface other people are mixed up just like you are? No offense."

"None taken. Call it a mutual understanding we extend to each other. And we don't talk about it, not even with newcomers. At least, not usually."

"Thanks, I think," Clint said, vaguely appreciative. But something felt off. True, he wanted to get home to see his family, but if the King was real, he had to honour his prayer to him. He had surrendered his life to Christ.

"What other people think is just half of it," he said. "It's what I feel when I fail that hurts the most. I can't stand letting the King down after all he's done for me."

"But that's the beauty of it. Focusing on the outward rules creates a kind of mask you can hide behind. Even when you look in the mirror. And you're doing the public things. That means you're checking off about half the list, right?"

"Does the mask thing work for you?"

"Mostly." She shrugged her shoulders dispassionately. "Here, I'll show you."

To Clint's astonishment, the woman peeled off her face. No, not her face. A mask that looked like her face with a plastic smile splitting it. It was right out of Mission Impossible. Her real face was scored by wrinkles etched by disappointment and sadness.

Apparently embarrassed to be seen without her mask, she quickly slipped it back on. In a few moments she'd stretched it back across her face and he couldn't tell she was wearing it. "There! See? That's better."

And actually, she did look better with the mask on. Sort of.

"Okay, but the King knows, doesn't he? If he's really Jesus and all that, he'll see right through this. How can you experience all the King's blessings if you can't be good enough to earn them? Isn't that what life here is all about?"

"To experience the King's gifts and blessings, you have to ask him. No one ever received without asking. And before you ask, you have to please him. Which is where the lists come in. And while you ask him, you have to use faith. Faith is basically stubbornness. The King wants you to press him. You have to find his promises in the book among the lists, and claim them for yourself."

"Claim them?"

"Write them down. Memorize them. Bring them up every time you talk to the King. Remind him to keep his promises, and persevere in your asking until he gives you what you ask for."

"He wants us to bother him?" Clint felt confused. "If he's real and he's here, why doesn't he just give us what we need?"

"He does, he does. But it usually takes some desperation. Some work. If you haven't received what you want, it's because you haven't asked passionately enough. Or because you need more devotional correctness. Or there may be sin in your life. Or some other issue. You'll see."

Clint felt dejected. It all sounded so complicated. "Is there a list of all that stuff?"

"Page 398."

He sighed again.

"No, no—there's no sense fighting it, Clint. That's how the King has designed his kingdom. It's the law."

"The law, huh? Well, if you say so. But does it actually work?"

"Not always." She shrugged her shoulders again. "Blessings come, blessings go. I guess you just kind of have to lower your expectations."

"That's not exactly why I surrendered to the King."

The woman's words felt like discouragement gnawing at his soul. For now, he was almost able to ignore it, even without a mask to help him. But he missed his girls terribly.

Chapter Three
The Pursuit

After his visitor left, Clint read a few more lists and then slammed the book shut extra hard, trying to muzzle his guilt. He felt like even walking out the door doomed him to failure, but then realized that staying put was letting the King down too. He opted for the indoor kind of failure because he wasn't ready to don one of those masks just yet, and failing in front of people felt worse somehow.

He almost stayed home from temple too, but then he had to get one thing right and the woman had mentioned that every good citizen of Basileia went to the temple thing. Plus, it was public, something people would notice, just like she'd recommended. Her excuses were beginning to work their magic on him.

Clint's spirits lifted some as he left his dwelling at seven p.m., which he hoped was early enough to get a good seat at Temple.

Apparently the giant building was situated on prime real estate on the back side of the mountain, conveniently just out of sight of the bridge, the chasm, and especially Kakos. They'd chosen a great location, really—no sense thinking about all those dying people in Kakos all the time. It made for a longer walk, but he needed the fresh air since he had opted to stay inside all day.

Slowly orbiting the mountain along the perimeter road, Clint noticed more and more people joining him on the walk. He also noticed the rooftops of the buildings on the level below, the so-called "new" city, and pondered what life might be like for people down there. Probably a lot like life where he was. He would have to ask his new friend about that.

He arrived at the temple just as the sun was giving up on the day, so he was glad for the lamplight inside. The building was obviously built to inspire awe. He was greeted at the door by friendly citizens who shook his hand heartily as he came in the door. He almost felt at home—almost—until he remembered his friend's disclosure. They were all modelling disguises, meaning he'd better play the part too.

With considerable effort, he began to smile broadly. In the end it wasn't so bad. With every step his face stiffened a little but his outlook brightened a few shades to compensate.

Clint had never seen such a big auditorium, which was cool, but his real joy was that he would finally see the King for himself. A large stone podium waited at the front of the room where he guessed King would stand to address them. As early as Clint was, he was still only able to find a seat halfway to the back. It wasn't the best seat in the house, but it gave him a decent view. Looking up, his jaw went slack. The auditorium had several levels, each with its own posh seating. He saw at least two more levels above him.

"I should probably get as high up as I can," he thought, leaving his seat for the upper levels. But after ten minutes of searching, it became obvious that there were no stairways from his level to the seating above him. Rushing back to the auditorium, Clint found himself sitting in one of the last remaining seats, right in the back. He kicked himself for giving up his first spot, but at least he was in.

As eight o'clock drew nearer, the buzz of temple conversations trailed off into a pious silence as a man dressed in a black robe paraded his way to the podium. Was this the King? The object of his heart's desire? Clint hoped not.

"Thank you all for coming. Bow your heads, and let us pray."

Clint didn't bow his head. The man obviously wasn't the King, so he didn't want to miss the moment when the real King took the stage. The man prayed and prayed—and prayed—but the King didn't appear. Near the end of the prayer, the man said, "Oh gracious King, we ask in your benevolent name that you would grace us with your presence today. Come, O King, and dwell among us. Come. We have left everything at the door— everything we have done, everything on our minds, everything that matters to us, and have come before you with empty hearts waiting for your breath to fill us."

Clint looked around. Still no King. But many of the people had raised their hands, stretching them out high into the air like naked tree branches in winter. It looked to Clint like they were begging for something.

Come, O King, the man had prayed. Did that mean the King was somewhere else? That perhaps he wouldn't come at all and had to be asked? What if they hadn't asked him properly? Or passionately enough? What if he was busy or out of the country?

Clint's heart slumped low and stayed there all the way through several songs that he didn't know, full of words he would have to look up later in the glossary of his new book. The melodies were okay—nothing like his radio station at home—but passable. Unfortunately they seemed hollow because they were about joy and peace and all kinds of things he didn't feel right then. Singing was part of the whole mask game, probably.

"Sing, sing your hearts out to the King," the song leader shouted. "The harder we sing, the more we will feel his presence. Come, O King, and dwell in our praises." Clint wondered how many people actually felt the King; he couldn't tell through their masks. But if singing enthusiastically regardless of how he was feeling was part of being a good citizen, so be it. Clint sang along.

Soon afterward, the man in black took the podium for a second time and began to speak. He opened an impressive copy of the Book of Duties—which was much larger than Clint's copy—and began to read. He dictated an inspiring story about the King, which made Clint pay closer attention. Finally, the story ended and the man looked up.

"We must all seek the King for ourselves." He closed the book with a holy thump. "If we seek him, we will find him."

"We must all seek the King for ourselves," the crowd said in unison, but Clint missed the moment and was the only one still repeating the words when the crowd fell silent. He blushed, and with that, the holy man was praying again.

"We thank you, O King, for being here with us today. Help us to be faithful citizens. Go with us now. In your name, amen."

Amen? But the King hadn't come at all. Clint was confused. Was temple a kind of mask too? Was the King even real? He had to be, if he was Jesus, but then what had just happened?

"Seek, seek, seek ..." the crowd said together. With that, they got up from their seats and dispersed into the night.

Clint shook his head, but still found himself curious about seeking the King. There was something to that, he decided. Perhaps it would help him keep the list, which would rack up the brownie points he needed to ask the King for his ticket home.

The next morning Clint awoke to the kitschy rooster again, slightly less startled than with the first offence but even more annoyed with the stupid creature. Clint realized once again that he'd slept in—apparently roosters in Basileia rose later than in other places. It was the bird's fault.

A moment later he cursed himself for missing his early morning appointment with the Book of Duties. Not a good start to the day. Snatching another apple, he held it with his teeth while tying the belt on his tunic, telling himself that he would get to his reading later on.

Pushing his guilt aside, he decided to wear a mask—for a day or two, tops—while he found his stride in Basileia. It was only temporary. When in Rome, do as the Romans do. His first priority was to find his merchant friend and ask her about that King-seeking business. So his 'church face' had a purpose after all.

Meandering past the park and down the street toward the riotous market, Clint noticed that a wall of clouds had painted the city in a mackerel grey. The crazy colours he'd seen on his first day had been replaced by a meh-faced palette. He reasoned that he must have been seeing the city through a naive optimism at first.

"Good morning." He beamed at his new friend when she looked up.

"Why, good morning." She winked at him. "I see you've found a mask to your liking. It suits you."

"Thank you, thank you." Clint dipped in a mock bow. "But I don't plan on wearing it for very long."

"Why, is it uncomfortable?"

"Uncomfortable, no. I actually forget I'm wearing it. But I'm here to talk to you about seeking the King. I think that's what I've been missing since I arrived."

"Ah, right you are."

"I thought so."

"But I'm not the one you need to talk to. Pop in on Simeon.

"Simeon?"

"He lives in the steep-roofed home and believe me, he's been seeking the King longer than any of us. If you want to properly begin the Pursuit, he's the one you should see."

"The Pursuit, huh? That's the seeking thing, right? I'll go see him."

"I'm Nomothesia, by the way." she said.

"What?"

"That's my name. Nomothesia."

Clint smiled. "Then thank you, Nomo…thesia." He would have to look that word up in the back of the book.

"You've been enjoying the apples I left you, haven't you?" She was teasing him.

Clint tipped his head. "Yeah, I have. How'd you know?"

"Your thirst for knowledge. That's what the fruit does. Which is good. the more we know, the more of the King's blessing we can enjoy."

It seemed true enough. The apples invigorated him, giving him a thirst for knowledge when he was discouraged. "Well, then, thanks again."

"You bet."

"And keep the apples coming."

"I will, I will."

Leaving the market behind, Clint sauntered into the suburb he'd seen on his first day in Basileia. Sure enough, one of the homes stood out from all the others with a roof pitched so steeply that it looked like a shingled rocket. The house of a true seeker. His ticket home.

He was about to knock on the front door when he noticed a note tacked to the wood.

"Out chasing down a sighting of the King in the park. I may be awhile." It was signed, "Simeon."

A sighting of the King? In the park? Clint charged back down the cobbled road as fast as his legs could take him. He passed a few other citizens also scampering in that direction. Maybe they'd caught a whiff of the rumour as well. He barrelled back through the market and jogged into a simple clearing in the park. A man was kneeling there, arms outstretched to the sky. Old man Simeon, apparently.

Clint was so excited to find Simeon that he barged right over to him, breathless and impatient. There was no King, but at least he was making progress. His words came out in bursts.

"I'm Clint ... Nomothesia said you could ... I want to find the King!"

"Oh, you just missed him." Simeon spoke cheerfully, though a smidgen of sadness lingered in the man's voice.

"Dude. You saw him?"

"Well, not exactly." Simeon lowered his arms and turned to face him. "But he was here. Look, his footprints are right there in the dirt."

Clint inspected the earth at Simeon's feet. An indistinct something had depressed some dirt in a few places but it was hard to make out. Clint never would have noticed the tracks if Simeon hadn't highlighted them.

"That's pretty subtle, bro. But I want you to teach me to seek the King. I want to see what you see."

"Ahhh, the great Pursuit," Simeon rubbed his hands together gleefully.

"Yeah, that."

"Walk with me and I will instruct you." The old man extended his hand to Clint, and he heaved Simeon to his feet.

"The King loves us, and we must love him in return," the sage explained as they strolled along. "We can't see him, but we must seek him anyway. He could be right with us now, in fact— invisible to our eyes."

"I think I understand. When the dude in the black robe at the temple was praying, I heard him asking the King to come into the service. I thought he never showed up, but maybe he did, in disguise or something."

"Yes, that's a common prayer. The King reigns high above us, so we must invite him to come down to be a part of our everyday lives."

"What if we forget to ask him? What if we don't seek him like we should?"

"Then I'm afraid we're on our own."

Clint nodded, then stopped. "But if you can't see him, how do you know if he's come?"

"He leaves his footprints and fingerprints for us to chance upon. Sometimes we recognize his whisper in the breeze, or catch a whiff of his sacred fragrance on the wind. And every so often—though you mustn't get your hopes up—he leaves us a note on the kitchen table to read."

Clint gasped. "Okay, you know what? He left me a note on the table the day I arrived."

"You see? The trick is to live for those moments, longing for the days when he appears to us, waiting for him to come down from above and touch our lives. The most noble citizens of Basileia are the most passionate seekers. And he rewards passion that's proven."

"I feel that passion right now," Clint said, breathless.

"I can see it on your face. You must put everything else in second place to that passion. You must seek the King with all your heart. If you seek him with all your heart, you will find him. Then and only then."

"Have you found him?" The question seemed to rock old Simeon.

"Well ... no. But I'm getting closer every day. You see, that's the secret. We all begin far away from the King. Keeping the list faithfully and seeking him, praying to him and reading the Book of Duties—all of these move us closer to him. Breaking the rules and not seeking the King pushes us away. He waits for faithful citizens to draw near, to pay the price for true intimacy with him."

"I want—no I need—to pay the price." Clint felt an adrenalized fire surging in his heart.

"I know you do." Simeon patted him on the shoulder. "But I must be off. Sometimes the King has been spotted at the southern well. It is my custom to go there in the afternoons just in case he passes by."

"Fair enough. Thanks for your help. Maybe I'll join you later. First I need to go home and study my Book of Duties."

"A wise choice. Make sure to memorize the verses. He likes that. You won't find him if he's not pleased with you."

And with that, Clint left Simeon to his Pursuit and marched off toward his temporary home. His stomach growled for another one of Nomothesia's apples.

Enflamed by Simeon's challenge, Clint spent the rest of the week fully engaged in the Pursuit. Every waking moment he thought about the King—asking him to come, foraging for clues, calling out his name, rushing off to places where the King had recently been. He pored over the Book of Duties every morning for half an hour, memorizing the parts that seemed important for proving his devotion. In the process he found several commanding truths he was certain would help him chance upon the King.

Even so, by the end of each day he still felt like he was one critical insight away from discovering the master principle that would clear up the mystery and guarantee his heart's desire. Unfortunately, every silver bullet seemed to misfire, leaving him no closer to finding his way home than the day he'd arrived.

Every day from dawn till way past bedtime Clint tried his best to comply with all the instructions on the lists. He spent hours memorizing the King's promises and transcribing them to bits of parchment. He waved them in the air as he prayed, reminding the King of his promises and claiming those blessings for himself. It was hard work, but he was sure he was becoming a better citizen. Certainly better than many of the people living around him.

It had to count for something.

Every once in a while Clint would catch a whiff of the King's scent on the night air or find a partial footprint in the soft earth. A couple of times he even found a short note from the King on his kitchen table. Clint longed to go home, but meeting the King would be amazing in and of itself.

Before long, Clint began to live for those fleeting moments when the King seemed to be near. It was as if the King was saying, "Keep looking. You're getting warmer." The King never used those words, of course, but how could he miss the message?

Unfortunately, most of the time the King did not seem nearer or warmer. In fact, most of the time it felt as if he were on some cosmic business errand infinite universes away, which left Clint feeling cold and empty.

The sporadic notes and hints vitalized him at first, but after a while it felt like the King was teasing him or playing hard to get. Near the end of the week he felt he was playing a giant game of cat and mouse—as though the King were dangling fresh clues just out of reach with no intention of letting Clint catch them. Hide and seek was a fun game to play but a terrible way to live.

Even worse, word got out that a few people in his neighbourhood had spent time with the King face to face that week. One family even hosted him for a late supper, then vanished along with him, apparently moving to another level he couldn't reach. What were they doing for the King that he wasn't? In the end he couldn't think of a single thing to do differently besides reading more of the Book of Duties and praying harder and longer.

So he did. But no matter how much progress he made in his devotional correctness, the King was nowhere to be found. Soon his frustration had frothed itself into a bubbling anger—all hidden behind his smiling mask, of course.

The mask had become a daily necessity by this time. He felt exposed and naked without the rubbery thing, only taking it off in the seclusion of his own home. He yearned to talk to Monica, wondering if he would ever see her or his precious Sarah again. He ached to go home, for life to return to normal.

How was he supposed to follow someone he couldn't see, hear, touch, feel, or find? If the King never showed up, how was that any different than being stood up? And how could he build a relationship with someone who was only around when he didn't notice?

Any hopes Clint had entertained of befriending the King or going home had been stretched so thin by now that they felt they might snap any second. Why would the King hide himself like this? Why would he withhold the key to his heart if he wanted to have a relationship with his subjects? It made no sense to him.

Rumour had it that the King lived at the top of the Mountain. After trying and failing at everything else, Clint decided that had to be the key. With his desperation deepening, Clint sold his home and found a tiny new one up on the Third Level—one step closer to the peak hidden by the clouds. He hoped this sort of bold move would count for something. In theory it would move him closer to the King and signal his unmatched devotion.

Higher and harder, that was his motto. But by the end of the third day in his new place the excitement of the move had evaporated and his new location didn't seem to matter. Still no King. It wasn't fair. He was more than paying the price for intimacy, but the King seemed oblivious to his dedication.

Fair or not, Clint couldn't ignore the aching pang in his soul. He often dreamt about drawing closer to the King and ached to connect with him heart to heart.

By now, though, his heart felt like a withering desert plant—and in weaker moments he thought of giving up the Pursuit for good. He was a failure at seeking the King and keeping his lists. He was a terrible citizen. How would he ever get home if he couldn't make the cut? Tears burned his eyes as he thought of Monica and Sarah wondering where he'd gone. As discouraged as he was, he would not, he could not, give up.

He figured he must still be missing something important. But what?

Chapter Four
The Spring of Thirst

The following Tuesday Clint left temple with heaviness blanketing his heart. He made no attempt to get anything meaningful out of the service. What did it matter? He was stuck in life, stuck in this stupid place. As he exited the auditorium, he saw Simeon milling around amongst the other believers.

"Hey Simeon."

Clint felt desperation rising like a lump in his throat. The man turned and gaped at him blankly.

"It's me, Clint." Simeon's eyes flickered in partial recognition. Apparently he was so zoned into pursuing the King that everyone else had faded from view.

"Yes, hello. How are you faring with the Pursuit?"

Clint sighed, not caring whether the man remembered him or not.

"Not so hot. I catch fleeting glimpses of the King, but mostly I see nothing, hear nothing, and feel nothing. Zippo."

"Well, do you feel empty inside?"

"Every single day."

"Marvellous. That's something." Simeon's eyes were gleaming.

"Marvellous?"

"Yes, yes. It means your heart belongs to the King. Without thirsting for him, without hungering deeply for his fellowship, you will never find him. Your'e getting closer."

"You're kidding, right?"

"Not at all. The most spiritual citizens in Basileia are the ones with the deepest thirst for the King. If we thirst for him, we will be satisfied by him. Eventually, at least."

Clint's mind began putting the pieces together.

"So, this city is like a living illustration of faith."

"No, this is real."

"Okay, but keeping the list and studying the Book of Duties every day is like the Second Level of Basileia."

"It's not *like* the second level. That's actually what we do on the second level."

"Ok, fine. But it's not enough, right? We need to do the Pursuit thing as the next step or whatever."

"Yes, that's it. Those who commit to the Pursuit ascend to the Third Level. Which is why, without even knowing why, you moved up to live in the Third Level of the city."

Clint's heart pounded in his chest. "Huh. I did move up here, didn't I? And it was my idea. So I'm on the right track?"

"Of course. But now that I know how serious you are, you should sell your home and move up to the Fourth Level. Of course, it will be a bit smaller there."

"I just got here." Clint's heart sank.

"Do you want to keep ascending the ladder into the King's grace? Do you still want to pay the price, no matter what the cost? The Book of Duties does say, "You shall love the King with all your heart, with all your mind, and with all your strength."

"I read that yesterday." Clint felt a faint hope flickering within him again.

"Come, come," Simeon said. "I'll show you to the Fourth Level."

"But my stuff ..."

"You can get your belongings later."

"Okay. Sure." Clint followed the doddering old man through the city streets until they reached another staircase, narrower than the first two and much steeper. He was sure Simeon would keel over and die right there on the stairs, but after a few dozen gasps and lurches they had spilled over onto the Fourth Level.

"I used to ... live here." Simeon put his hands on his hips, trying to catch his breath. "But as you can see, my legs ... and lungs ... aren't what they used to be."

"The Fourth Level sure is smaller than the Third."

"And the Fifth is smaller still. The path narrows as we near the King, and fewer live at each level because fewer citizens are willing to sell all to have the pearl."

"The pearl?"

"Look it up in the book. Come, follow me."

Simeon led Clint along the ring road, and before long they had found a whimsical neighbourhood a little smaller than the one he had left behind and far more modest. Nothing was dressed up or refined like in the Second and Third Levels. Clint guessed those living on the Fourth Level were so passionate about the King that shiny new stuff didn't tempt them anymore.

It didn't take the pair long to locate Clint's new dwelling, a fresh two- bedroom apartment overlooking the lower levels, the bridge, the chasm, and the city of Kakos sulking in the distance. It had been awhile since he had thought about the dark city.

Simeon saw Clint staring out the window. "Kakos," he said.

"Yeah," Clint replied. "When I arrived, the dance troupe said we all come from there."

Simeon joined him at the window. He stood there for a long breath before responding. "They were speaking the truth."

"How did I ... I mean, how do people ..."

"How is it that people living in Kakos come to live in Basileia? They must give their heart to the King. You know that."

"But how are they supposed to find out about the King?"

"We have to tell them. We have to reach out to them."

"But since I've been here, no one has talked much about that. Should we be crossing the bridge over into Kakos to talk to them? Maybe host a barbecue or something? I do this killer pork marinade."

"Heavens, no." Simeon shuddered. "Foolish renegades from the New City often go there, but no one in the Old City would even dream of such a thing. If Kakosians want to come to Basileia, they can come to us. We send them invitations to attend temple every week, but they rarely choose to come. Their loss."

Clint barely heard Simeon's last sentence. "What about the New City?"

"The New City? For dreaming idealists. Did you know that the entire New City sits on the lower level of Basileia, set below our very First Level?" He rolled his eyes. "Think how far they live from the peak. Think about how much closer to the King you are."

"It was brighter down there." Clint felt his face stiffen with sadness.

"That's because we're ascending into the clouds, Clint."

"That makes no sense. Maybe they aren't clouds. Maybe it's like a fog. I had forgotten until now, but in his first note, the King said something about meeting him in the New City. I should try that."

Simeon sighed. "You have so much to learn." He grabbed Clint's sleeve and led him away from the window. Both Clint and Simeon gasped as they passed through the kitchen. There was another note centred on the tabletop, set next to a crystal goblet full of sparkling water. The sight made Clint's heart dance.

Clint, I miss you. Please enjoy this drink, on me. It will refresh your spirit. When are you coming to the New City? I'm waiting for you there.

~ The King

"Ha. See? I told you, he misses me." Clint waved the note in Simeon's face. "And he mentioned the New City again. He wants me to visit him there. I'm totally going."

Simeon's countenance darkened. He shook his head slowly. "It's a trick."

"A trick? Come on."

The old man strode over to the window. He pulled the shades to cover the opening. "Come to temple on Tuesday and you will see."

"But Simeon, read it yourself. The King ..."

"Trust me. Do nothing rash until you hear the preacher. He will help you understand. And whatever you do, don't even think of drinking this water."

Clint was confused. "Why not?"

"If the note is a fake, the drink may well be poisoned. Think, Clint. Why would the King give you a goblet of his royal water when you're living on the Fourth Level, the very place where his Spring of Thirst flows free for all to drink?"

"I don't know. Maybe ..."

"Perhaps I should get you to the well. One sip of that water will show you the truth."

Clint let his shoulders slump. "So the note isn't really from the King?"

"I'm afraid not." Simeon patted him on the shoulder. "The enemy counterfeits the King's gifts all the time. Most miracles are counterfeits, in fact."

Clint felt too dejected to argue. "Fine. Just take me to the well then."

He didn't have to wait long. The seven-tiered fountain sat not five minutes from his apartment. Majestic pillars flanked the central pool, which was now surrounded by a hundred people excitedly drawing water into cups, urns, buckets, and even flagons.

"Behold, the Spring of Thirst." Simeon grinned, waving his arms theatrically.

"It's pretty cool," Clint said, just as much to himself as to Simeon.

"Drink, drink."

"Can I? I mean, is it free?"

"Of course it's free. Haven't you read? We may come and drink and have our fill at no cost."

"I guess I haven't gotten that far in the book yet. " Clint stepped carefully toward the sensational pool, while Simeon shoved his way through thirsty pilgrims until he had found the edge. He bent over the railing suddenly, tipping himself forward until his feet left the ground and his lips met the surface. He drank deeply and his body shuddered with apparent delight. Rocking himself back up to a standing position, he wiped his mouth with his sleeve, grinning from ear to ear.

"Drink, Clint. Drink."

Clint needed no further encouragement. Bending over as his new mentor had, he leaned in close until he could test a tiny sip's worth. It was delicious.

"What do you think?" Simeon clapped his hands in childlike delight. "Well?"

Clint had to think for a moment. Then another. "It tastes like ... like…"

"Like what?"

"Like more." Clint plunged his entire face into the pool, drinking as fast as he could take it in without choking.

Over the next few days Clint found himself returning often to the fountain for refills of the King's water. By the end of the week he could hardly go two hours without the stuff. Between

Nomothesia's magic apples and the Spring of Thirst he could barely contain his swelling passion for fellowship with the King.

Funny enough, his new thirst produced a welcome side effect—he never missed his daily appointment with the Book of Duties. His appetite for the lists grew with his thirst, and his devotional correctness became more consistent. He fasted one meal a day, enjoyed retreats of silence, and even memorized large chunks of the book. He was on his way to pleasing the King and earning his ticket home. He could feel it.

True, he didn't see or hear the King at all, but he was sure his devotion would pay off sooner or later. Clint decided that when the King came calling, he would find him both thirsty and faithful. The only drawback was that he had lost some weight and felt weaker than he had in a long time. But that didn't matter. If his fasting and prayer pleased the King, it was a small price to pay. His family was worth it.

The night before temple, Clint sat back in his new bed, relishing the joy filling his heart. Who would have thought that thirsting for the King would be the key to growth in his kingdom? True, the King had promised all who came to him would be satisfied, but Clint now saw that the promise was about the bliss between drinks, not satisfaction as a way of life.

Clint could hardly wait for the upcoming temple gathering. Trying to quiet himself, he finally gave up on sleeping. He tiptoed out the front door to make his way back to the pool for another drink, trying not to disturb his neighbours. To his surprise, at least twenty people were already there, every one turning to grin at him sheepishly under the full moon.

"Thirsty, huh?" A young boy stood before him.

Clint wondered where the kid's parents were. "You bet, partner. That's why I'm here."

A teenage girl was also enjoying the pool. She wasn't shy either. "It's amazing, isn't it? The more you drink, the more you need. The more you want the King. I feel like I'd die without this way of life."

"I've been coming here for ten years and I still can't get enough," a middle-aged man said, joining the conversation. "It satisfies you and intensifies your thirst at the same time."

Clint looked over at the man and smiled, but when he looked closer, his smile evaporated. "Hey man, are you okay?"

"Me? Sure. I'm just thirsty. Thirsty for the King."

But the man didn't look thirsty. He looked deathly sick, or like a rotting walker on the set of The Walking Dead. Deep hollows hung around his eyes. Clint recoiled at the sight.

"Uh, dude? Just out of curiosity, when was the last time you saw the King?" he asked the man.

"Personally? I haven't seen him in years."

"Not for *years*?" Clint was shocked. "And you're proud of it? I thought thirsting for the King would please him. That he would reveal himself to us more often."

"Then you've misunderstood."

"But I have to get home." Clint felt faint. "I need my family. I ..."

"Home? This is home, friend. Get used to it."

"But I thought ..."

"How do you make someone thirsty? By satisfying them? No, by depriving them. By starving them. By keeping water from them."

"But he's given us the spring," Clint said.

"To make us thirsty, friend. This isn't really water, you know. Real water would quench our thirst." The man looked insane in the otherworldly moonlight. His eyes were dead, bulging from his gaunt frame.

Clint's heart pounded. "What? I don't—"

"It's true! Water would quench our thirst. But then we wouldn't thirst for the King, would we? And what would be the good of that? You're more spiritual now than you've ever been." The man's voice grew louder as he spoke. "Take a good look at yourself, friend. You're a gaping hole."

Glancing down at his reflection in the pool, Clint choked. It was true. He saw a zombie, a walking skeleton. It was then that he noticed his lips. They were cracked and misshapen. His arms were rotting and weak. His scalp smouldered with fear. What was wrong with him? Stumbling back from the fountain, he lost his balance and then flopped onto his backside.

Clint fought for breath as his heart pattered and faltered. Stars began to dance before his eyes. He had to get back to his apartment, to calm down, to rest. Pushing himself to his feet, he forced himself to move. All he could manage was a tottering, dizzy gait across the uneven stones. It was stubborn fear alone that managed to drive him back to his dwelling without fainting.

The moment he stepped inside, his legs gave way and he sprawled onto all fours. Staring at the tan tiles and gasping for breath, Clint tried to command his withered muscles. It was only with the greatest effort that he was able to wrangle his feverish body onto his cot. Shivering there in the dark, he tried to pray.

"King, I don't understand. I'm thirsty for you, just like you wanted. I'm reading my book faithfully. I'm learning to keep the lists. I'm seeking you all day long and fasting and praying. I'm going to temple every week."

Breaking down completely, Clint began to sob. "I just want to go home. Help me, King. Just let me go. Please."

It was then that he remembered the bogus note and the goblet on the kitchen table. Simeon had insisted it was a fake, that the liquid in the cup was poison. But Clint didn't care. If it was poison, he would drink to his misery. Maybe then this nightmarish religion would finally end and he would wake up in bed at home.

After rolling himself off the cot, he heaved his stiffening body across the cold floor, eventually reaching the kitchen. Pulling together a last reservoir of strength, he propped himself up and paused to catch his breath. The goblet was still there on the table. Snagging the cup with the tips of his trembling fingers, he slid it slowly toward himself, then brought it to his lips. Time to end the journey.

Clint downed the whole thing in a few clumsy gulps. A few seconds later he felt his mind slipping away. He embraced the blackness.

Chapter Five
Battle

Clint awoke at suppertime the following day, pleased by how refreshed and content he felt. He lay there on the floor for a long time, both getting his bearings and wondering if the episode at the fountain the night before had only been a nightmare. His skin crawled as he remembered his conversation with the sickly middle-aged man, his undead reflection in the water, and the frantic journey back to the apartment.

It was then that he noticed his front door had been left wide open. He also saw the King's goblet lying on its side beside him on the floor. The nightmare had really happened.

But he was also alive. And somehow at peace. The King's water? That had to be it. Holding up his hand to his face, he was dumbfounded at the sight. His fingers were pink, his palm was meaty, and his arm was no longer skeletal. Touching his face, he tried to trace the contour of the deep hollows he had found there the night before and felt only a full, blushing cheek filling his hand.

Clint began to cry. Slapping the tiles euphorically, he also began to laugh. The joy came so hard that his sides hurt, so fast that he couldn't breathe. It wasn't long before tears glazed his face and he wasn't sure whether he was laughing, crying, or both. When the outburst had run its course, he looked up at the ceiling, smiling.

"Thank you. That was an amazing gift. I'm going to go down to the New City today. I just have to..."

His prayer was interrupted by a bawdy trumpet blast. A moment later it sounded again. Soon he could hear people running through the streets. A loud pom-pom-pom sound joined the mayhem. Someone was clobbering a drum so hard that his heart jumped at the cadence. What was going on?

After bouncing to his feet, he stumbled to the open doorway just as a muscle-bound soldier was marching by. Spying Clint, he stopped to address him.

"Don't stand there looking dumb as a doorpost. Where's your armour, soldier?" Spittle sprayed as he spoke.

"Uh, I'm not a soldier, so…" Clint found himself retreating a step or two into his apartment.

"What?" The man's veins were bulging like angry balloons from his neck. "Every citizen of Basileia is a soldier. Every citizen must fight. And we're at war, in case you hadn't heard."

Clint felt the blood drain from his newly blushed cheeks. War? He couldn't believe it. "Isn't this a peaceful kingdom? I don't …"

The impatient soldier stomped up to him, grabbed him by the scruff of his neck, and hauled him like a rebellious child into the middle of the street. The strong arms spun him around to face the direction of Kakos. "Look for yourself, boy."

Clint did look. He saw the giant cloud hanging over mournful Kakos as usual. This morning, however, the haze was moving, advancing toward them, drawing nearer every moment. Except it wasn't a haze. It was an army, maybe a thousand winged creatures of pooling blackness were flapping toward Basileia in battle formation. The Old City's collective dread was palpable.

"Unless you want to get eaten alive, I suggest you haul yourself to the temple and slap your armour on," the soldier said, letting Clint go. "And take up your sword. I expect to see you on the front lines. Got it? We need every body bearing arms."

Clint nodded, mesmerized by the advancing maelstrom. He'd never been at war before—or held a sword, or shot a bow, or swung anything heavier than a badminton racket. This wasn't a video game. He had to get himself to the temple and figure out what to do. Or where to hide.

After scrambling back and forth frantically for ten minutes Clint realized there was no entrance into the temple from Level Four. He decided to brave his way up to the Fifth Level.

The path had been chiseled out from a cliff wall and climbed more like a ladder than a stairway. Once he reached the top, Clint took a moment to get his bearings. The Fifth Level was the smallest of all, housing less than half of the population scrunched into the level he'd come from.

Every citizen he saw was either decked out in full armour or marching toward the temple—apparently to get outfitted. He joined the marchers and within a few minutes found himself standing in a lineup of grim Basileians waiting for their gear. A tall man stood behind the desk, wiping stray droplets of sweat from his eyes. His hands were trembling.

Clint noticed piles of armour covering the greasy counter— one for helmets, one for swords, and a few more—breastplates, girdles, and boots. He picked up a dented helmet from its pile.

"How much?"

"It's free, compliments of the King."

"So ..."

"One of each, and please keep moving."

"Okay, but..."

"One size fits all, sir." He drew out his syllables to sound condescending. The man's fuse was clearly burning out. Not wanting to cause a scene, Clint loaded his arms full of armour and perched the sword on top. The stuff was heavy. He wondered if he would be able to move once he'd put it on.

Clint felt totally awkward and confused. What was he supposed to do? He found a regal knight already outfitted for battle and worked up the courage to ask the warrior a question.

"Did I miss the sermon today? I didn't even see a place for seating in there."

"Seating?" The man laughed a tin laugh behind his visor. "This is battle level, boy. Kill or be killed. Learn as you go. Moses had time for prayer, but Joshua was a man of steel. If I were you, I'd get that armour on pretty quick. And do it every day without fail. The diabolon are upon us."

The soldier gripped his sword and lunged for cover under an overhanging roof. Seconds later the air vibrated with a howling that could have been heard from miles away. But they, whatever they were, were closer than that. Much closer. The air crackled with dark power.

The soldier was shouting now. "Run, man. And keep your shield up."

A moment later a cold shadow snaked across the ground in front of him. A coal-black lion with a snow-white mane and cruel reptilian wings was circling the rooftops above them. Clint found himself stunned into silence.

Soon two diabolon were circling. Then three. After dropping his helmet in fear, Clint turned and bolted for a nearby alleyway, bumbling into cover with his bundle of armour just as the roaring creature streamed past. The knight across the street was bellowing at him again. "Your helmet, you crazy fool. You're a dead man without your helmet!"

Without thinking, Clint darted back out onto the street and plucked his helmet from the hot dust. The dark shadow poured like lava across the stones as a massive diabolos dropped from the sky at him, roaring so loudly it made his chest shudder. He threw himself back into the alleyway just as the thing flapped past. A near miss.

Clint clutched at his helmet with stupid fingers and clumsily pushed the piece on. Jumping into the breastplate on the ground, he yanked it up as fast as he could but found it difficult to secure the leather straps with his sweaty fingers. It didn't help that all around him the diabolon were flapping and thundering and people were screaming at the top of their lungs.

Glancing down the street, Clint saw a line of knights trying to mount a counter-attack.

"For the King!" they cried. He watched the brave garrison advance on two diabolon who had made a stand in the middle of the street. He shook his head as he realized two of the knights were mere children. One was an older woman. They swung their swords wildly at the monsters, mostly tracing air.

The diabolon were not intimidated. Serrated fangs bared, the giant cat-dragons circled the knights, growling and snarling with rage, throbbing for an outlet. One beast lunged forward, teeth snapping. It locked its massive jaws over a man who hesitated half a second too long in one place. Flipping the hapless warrior into the air like a chunk of meat, the thing's mouth distended unnaturally as it devoured him—armour and all.

The second monster lashed out with its formidable paws, slamming the woman so hard that she cannonballed across the street and pounded through a wooden porch. She could not have survived the blow.

The horrific sights froze Clint's mind momentarily. This was insane! Where was the King? Who would defend them against this attack? He noticed that the knights were now retreating. One was limping toward his alley, dragging a badly mangled leg behind him.

"Are you all right?" Clint asked, concerned.

"Long live the King."

As the man spoke, Clint winced at the sight of his blood-flecked teeth.

"Does this happen often?"

"The war, you mean? Daily. It's a moment by moment crusade every true citizen of Basileia must embrace with courage."

"Daily? How come I haven't seen this before?"

"Because you weren't spiritual enough. Our enemy whispers in our thoughts. He brings us sickness and tempts us to abandon the Pursuit. He attacks us with ruthless evil every day of our lives and can be lurking anywhere. For all I know, you might be one of his dark allies. The only way to survive is to fight back with everything the King provides."

"But who are you—I mean we—fighting?"

"Pythus, serpent king of Kakos. Our true enemy."

"Why doesn't the King do something about this Pythus creature?" Clint asked, still horrified by the raging beasts terrorizing the city.

"Oh, he has. Many years ago, when the bridge between Kakos and Basileia was completed, he marched to Kakos and overcame Pythus and the diabolon all by himself. His victory gives us a place to stand today in battle. His victory is our victory."

Clint looked down at the knight's leg, still bleeding critically.

"It doesn't look like you're winning, or ever could for that matter. Those monsters are huge."

"A glorious day is coming when our final victory will come, but until then, we must engage the enemy and use the armour and weapons the king gives us to defeat our foes."

"I thought you said they were already defeated."

"Correct."

"But then ..." Clint had barely uttered the words when his mind registered the sound of a lion thing breathing to his left. A single diabolos was at the mouth of the alleyway, its eyes narrowed by volcanic hatred.

The knight let his shield drop to his knees. "It must have sniffed out a chink in my armour. They can smell weakness. I need more prayer support. More fasting. More prayer. Don't make my mistake."

"We can smell much more than weakness," the diabolos cackled. "Your carelessness ushers in your death. Your flesh will be my feast."

Astoundingly, the soldier offered no resistance to the bloodthirsty creature as it charged into the alley, thrashing him against the wall like a plaything. Clint looked away as it pulled the man apart.

Spinning around to run, Clint noticed too late that he'd backed himself up against the railing overlooking Level Four. As the beast charged with gaping jaws, he was ploughed over the edge and careened into space. His only thought was that if he died now, he would never see his girls again. Clint's scream was cut short by a punishing impact a moment later.

Chapter Six:
Crash

Throbbing pain rippled through Clint's neck, back, and hips, joined by the fierce ringing in his ears.

The diabolos had flipped him off the Fifth Level and he had fallen. Fallen where? To the Fourth Level, apparently. And he wasn't dead, at least not yet. Grimacing at the pain he felt when he tried to move, he decided to stay put for the time being.

The dead sky stared blankly at him through a hole in a thatched roof, which Clint guessed had saved his life by breaking his fall. The armour had probably helped too, though the back of his head had a nasty bump on it. Half expecting a diabo-thing or even Pythus himself to crash through the opening at any moment to finish him off, he tried to stop his heart from pounding.

The final attack never came. In fact, all the sounds and screams of battle were gone. He'd been left for dead. How long had he been unconscious? Wiggling his toes, he ruled out broken legs. Next he rotated each arm, relieved that they were in working order too. His back was badly bruised, but with concerted effort he managed to roll into a sitting position among the nest of straw and mortar he had dragged down with him on his way through the roof.

Next he removed his helmet, now rank and damp from the sweat and heavy breathing of battle. This helped quell the ringing in his ears a little, but he felt a chill run through his body as the evening air spilled into his armour.

With some effort and a whole lot of pain, Clint managed to strip off the clumsy iron. He stood leaning against an interior wall, breathing hard. An empty goblet lay on its side on the floor beside the table.

No freaking way.

He'd landed in the middle of his home on the Fourth Level. He started to smile, then wrenched his face into a scowl. Was there no escape? A fresh basket of Nomothesia's apples was arranged quaintly on the kitchen table. The sight made him furious. He batted it into oblivion with the back of his hand and stormed out of the house.

Clint railed at the King and the blank sky. "I want my life back. Following you is too much work. I can't feel you, I can't see you, and I just about got myself killed trying to follow you. So thanks a lot!"

Marching down the road toward the stairwell, he kept up his rant. "This can't be what faith is about. If it is, I think I'll stop caring so much. Ignorance sounds like bliss. Well, maybe not bliss, but it's better than locking horns with Pythus all day. Ooh, wait, maybe this doubt is just the diabolon at work, baiting me again. Maybe I've fallen prey to their sinister devices."

He laughed manically. "Uh oh. I'd better check my armour for holes I've overlooked. Or pump out some more promise prayers. Or reclaim my blessings before they're gone for good. Or am I already too late?" Growling to himself, he climbed the steep stairs back down to the Third Level.

"I know what I should do. I should starve myself some more, just in case you've withdrawn from me because of some awful sin I'm not aware of. Better safe than sorry, I guess. Right? Right?"

Clint paused, waiting for the King to answer. "Sorry, I forgot how busy you are and how small I am compared to you. I guess I had it coming, though. Apparently I haven't memorized enough of your precious book to earn another note on the table. Maybe another ten minutes a day would do the trick. Or is it twenty? Tell you what, keep changing the rules on me. I love guessing games."

Clint began to run. "While I'm waiting, maybe I should line up with Simeon at the fountain of death for my daily refill of salt water. That's always good for a laugh. I love zombie humour."

People were staring at him, horrified, but he didn't care. "You should try it too, everyone. Maybe we all should. Drink up, you sorry, stupid followers. And anyway, the Walking Dead is cool, right? You can all be extras next season."

Shouting at them didn't help, but the bitterness of his soul was churning to the surface and he was not about to censor it this time. Something had snapped within him, broken deep inside. His hope had crumpled, his faith had shattered, and he wanted out. He descended the stairs to the Second Level.

"Hey quick—someone hand me another list! Oh, and a mask. One with a bigger, whiter smile." His voice sounded shrill now, like a banshee's. He didn't care.

"You know what I need? More guilt. More failure. More to do, more to kill my heart. Why on earth would I want to see my wife again? Or my Sarah? I don't miss them at all. In fact, I'd rather die here any day with all of you. Who wouldn't?" He was sobbing now, and he choked on his tears.

Nomothesia stood in front of him, gripping her cart nervously.

"Clint, what's wrong?" She moved toward him, arms extended with motherly sympathy.

"What's wrong? What's not? And by the way, your pretty little mask is on crooked. I can see your sins plain as day." He shook his fist at the onlookers.

"Oops. I wasn't supposed to say that, was I? Did I break the code? Oh well. But I can see you, everyone. I can see all of your sins. Every single juicy one of them." He heard himself screaming, and his arms waved in threatening circles to match.

Nomothesia's face went slack but he didn't care. He sprinted past her, pushing his tortured body beyond its ability to keep up. By the time he'd found the final staircase to the main level he was hyperventilating badly. Halfway down the stairs, he began to see stars.

"Old City or New City?"

The toothless lump of a guard was still there, doing his special job— handing out the Book of Despair to people who didn't know any better. He bowled the man over with extra gusto, sending the brainless greeter sprawling headlong over a neat stack of his shiny new books.

Clint tried to blink away the darkness, but he couldn't stop it. The blackness was dripping like psychic tar into his soul.

"Strike me dead, King whoever-you-are. I dare you." But nothing happened. "No? Do you need more blasphemy? More anger? What... do you... want?"

Stumbling out the front gate of the accursed city, Clint vaguely recalled the gravelly path slipping away from his feet and the ground flying up to meet him. His face slapped the stones and everything went black.

CHAPTER SEVEN:
AWAKENING

Over the next few hours Clint's mind registered several confusing sensations: being dragged across gravel, bouncing and jiggling, and recently, the sweet aroma of freshly baked bread.

It was the bread that finally coaxed him from his stupor. That, and the singing. A woman was in the room with him, humming some kind of tune under her breath. He kept his eyes closed, opting to fake sleep until he had determined what was going on. The singing was his first clue. Nomothesia? No, the voice was all wrong.

Clint instantly recalled the harsh words he had spoken to his friend and regretted even opening his mouth. Another stupid failure. Whatever spiritual mineshaft he had fallen into was his own problem. She'd meant nothing but good from the moment he'd met her and didn't deserve the disrespect he'd slapped her with.

On the other hand, he wasn't sure he wanted to see her again either. Like, ever. For one thing, he found himself nauseated by just thinking about the Book of Duties. The guilt it had dumped on his soul was asphyxiating. Feeling around in his tunic, he was quite relieved to discover he had dropped the thing somewhere along his manic descent. Good riddance. He just wanted to go home.

Opening his eyes just a crack, he indulged in a slow pan of the room from right to left. A quaint little cottage of some kind with a round woman kneading a large ball of dough several feet away.

To the left... he snapped his eyes shut as they fell on a smallish figure sitting next to him. A little girl watching him like a hawk. And giggling.

"I saw you peeking. How'd you sleep?"

Clint wouldn't have classified passing out as sleep. It had been more like a religion-induced coma. But he couldn't exactly say that, so he opened his eyes and managed a weak smile.

"Okay I guess."

At his voice the woman turned to him, smiling warmly. "Well, hello. I see you've awakened, and my goodness—you look better already." She stood up and craned her neck out a tiny window over the sink. "Vita, our guest is awake." She saw Clint raising an eyebrow and understood. "I'm Rosa, and Vita is my husband. He found you curled up in the fetal position outside the wall."

Clint blushed with humiliation. "Oh, lovely."

"None of that." It was a gentle scolding, but then she slipped him an unpretentious smile. "That's where he found me a couple of years ago."

Clint raised his eyebrows.

"Yup. It's true," the little girl said, piping in.

"Our daughter, Shelah," Rosa explained.

The front door screeched on its hinges, wobbling inward to make room for a giant man who had to duck an inch just to get through the doorway. The woman motioned proudly toward him.

"My Vita."

Vita's blue eyes sparkled. "And I see you've met Rosa." He strode over to Rosa, lodging an affectionate kiss on her cheek. Now it was her turn to blush.

"Are you well, friend? Can you walk?" Vita asked Clint.

"My back hurts. And my head, and elbow. My whole life hurts, come to think of it. But who are you, exactly?"

"I'd like to show you instead of telling you," Vita replied.

"So... can you walk?"

"I guess so."

"Here, this will help." Rosa tore off a generous chunk of the fresh bread that had wooed him from his melancholy stupor and handed it to him.

"Thank you," he said, remembering his despair. "But I have to get going."

"I found you outside of the city, friend." Vita was frowning with apparent concern. "Where have you come from? Where were you going?"

Clint sighed for what felt like the millionth time since he had entered Basileia. "Apparently I came from Kakos, hallelujah, but during the past few weeks I've been giving it a go here in Basileia. I was on my way back out when you found me."

"Back to Kakos? But why?" The child's eyes looked like eggs ready to hatch.

"No, not to Kakos. Back... home. But if I can't get home, then back to Kakos, onto the bridge, or maybe a swan-dive to the bottom of the chasm. At this point, I could care less."

He let his eyes drop to the floor. "I'm done with Basileia and the Pursuit. I'm done with the King. With everything. No offense." Glancing up at Vita, he noticed his host's eyes were brimming with tears. "Oh, hey, I'm sure all this is good for you guys. But like I said, I'm done. Kaput."

"You've been staying in the Old City, haven't you?"

"Most people do. The guy at the gate said so."

"You don't have to be defensive. What Vita means is that the Old City is all over your face," Rosa said.

"My face?"

"Your mask."

Shelah stepped closer to Clint and took his face in her tiny hands before he could pull away. She stood there until he had worked up the courage to return her gaze. She looked and even smelled like his daughter, little Sarah. Her voice melted his bitterness—but only a little.

"Can I take it off?"

"Well, I guess it must be pretty beat-up by now." Shame dragged down his shoulders like a heavy yoke, but Shelah was waiting for his reply.

"Sure. Fine. Have at 'er."

"This doesn't even fit you anymore, silly," she said, tenderly peeling the stubborn layer off inch by inch.

When she was done with it she held the skin at arm's length like it was some kind of dead animal she'd found in the yard. She quickly passed it to Vita, who flung the sticky mess into the fire. It bubbled and contracted for a minute, then burst into flames.

"Good riddance," Rosa said.

"Your real face is much nicer. But you look so sad. Don't be sad." Shelah was staring into his eyes, searching for something. And for the first time since he'd met her, her eyes looked sad too. A lump started climbing his throat and he tried to chase it down again.

"Yeah, I guess I need a new mask. I'll get right on that."

"No you don't."

"I really should be going."

"You should stay." Rosa put her hand gently over his. "Don't write off Basileia until you have lived awhile in the New City."

"The New City?" Clint felt his upper lip quiver. "The King mentioned the New City in some of his notes to me."

"The New City is his home," Vita said, gesturing to the world outside.

"And it's yours, if you'd like it to be," Rosa added.

"Uh no. I mean, no thank-you. The Old City fools said the King lived there too, but I never saw him. Not even once."

"Please stay with us. He can stay, right, Mama?"

Shelah wiped away a tear that had slipped from his eyes. But just as suddenly as he felt himself soften, he steeled himself, hardening his heart into granite. He stood up suddenly, breaking free of the embrace. His head spun with confusion.

"No. Look, I've tried every level this city has to offer. I've followed the pretty little rainbow you people seek all your lives, right to the very end, right to the top, right into the clouds even. I did the Pursuit, the Spring of thirst, battle level, everything. I was all in. And you know what? It led me to nothing but a gaping hole in my soul. I think I've lost what little faith I had to begin with, and I may never see my family again. So like I said, I'm done."

"I don't know about your family, but you haven't tried the New City." Vita's voice was firm.

"I told you, I'm done trying," Clint replied, his voice even firmer. "I don't need any more levels. I've got to find a way to get home."

"I agree," Vita said. "You don't need any more levels."

"You only need a little bit of something new," Shelah piped in.

"A little what? A new quest? A little list to memorize?"

"A little faith," she said. "A little seed of faith is big enough to move the mountain. To get rid of it forever."

He tried to smile at her. "Thank you. Really. But I have to go."

Vita sighed, gesturing toward the door. "Then we won't stop you."

"It's nothing personal, guys. I've just had my hopes dashed too many times to count. Too often to recover from. I need to walk away, at least for now. I'll find my own way home somehow or other."

"I understand." Rosa was smiling through tears. The look in her eyes told Clint she was telling the truth. Under different circumstances he would have liked to hear her story, but the awkwardness was palpable. Nodding to Vita as he stepped out of the cottage, he braced himself for a second journey out of the accursed city.

Clint lifted his eyes to chart his path and stopped cold. cry escaped his lips before he could even react. He stumbled back through the door. Vita, Rosa, and Shelah were standing there grinning, arms crossed, apparently waiting for him to return.

"It's ... it's ..."

"We know."

Vita extended a burly hand to Clint. "Care to take that walk now, friend?"

"Here, take some more bread." Rosa stuffed a chunk into his palm just before Vita led him out the front door into a whole new world.

The King's world.

Chapter Eight:
The Book of Life

Clint felt like a little kid visiting Disneyland, the ocean, the mountains, and his grandparent's cabin at the lake for the first time—all at the same time. He walked through the New City as if he were in a trance, trying to take in the wonders around him. He stretched out a tingling hand. The air felt alive, shimmering and twinkling. It looked like exquisitely small golden snowflakes were suspended weightless before them. As he moved his hands, the stuff swirled like liquid, brightening momentarily wherever his hands made contact with the particles.

"What… is it?"

Vita smiled warmly, obviously enjoying the look on Clint's face. "The air of the kingdom. The glory of the King. His kingdom is a realm of light, of glory, of life."

"This is so cool," Clint replied, mesmerized at the sight. "Is it always here, or does it come and go?"

"The kingdom is a real place, Clint. Many people forget that. A kingdom begins with a King, as you know. In the Old City, the kingdom is all about keeping the rules and effort and striving. But there can't be a kingdom without a realm. The King's realm includes the space in our hearts given over to him, but it's far more than that. The truths in the King's book aren't just pretty words or ideas. You have entered a real kingdom, a realm of splendour and light. Bask in its glow. Breathe it in."

"I'm up for that."

The big man laughed. "I thought you were done."

Clint put on his best cheesy smile. "So… when I said I was 'done,' I didn't mean 'done-done.' I meant… uh…"

"Done with the Old City."

"Right. That. But Vita, you mentioned the King's book. I think I lost mine. Or chucked it." Clint felt a pang of regret at the thought. But it was too late now.

"Is this it?" Vita slipped a book from behind his back. Clint thought he recognized the worn brown cover immediately, but the title was different.

"No," he said finally. "Thanks though."

"I found it right next to you by the Gate."

"My book was a Book of Duties."

"I supposed it was."

"And this one is a Book of Life."

"At this moment, yes."

Clint was confused. "Then it isn't mine."

"King, help me to explain this to my friend."

"Pardon me?"

"I was talking to the King."

"Praying, you mean. Been there, done that. But not anymore."

"You haven't truly prayed until you've prayed from within the New City," Vita explained. "I also assure you that this is your book."

"No, it's got the wrong name. This one says 'The Book of Life.' Mine was a "Book of Duties."

"I know. But the book is alive, Clint."

"Alive?"

"Yes. It contains the breath and life of the King. But all living things adapt to their surroundings, so when we touch the book our personality mingles with the message. We tend to see it as we are, not as it is. Look at the book again." He gave it to Clint.

Clint looked again. He cocked his head at the sight, confused. "The Book of Duties."

"Is it?"

"Sure. Look for yourself. The letters clearly say so on the cover." Clint handed the volume back to Vita. A moment later, the big man shook his head in disagreement.

"No. It's a Book of Life. See?" Sure enough, the letters now spelled "The Book of Life," just as they had a minute earlier.

"Whoah. Is this some kind of trick?"

"Not a trick. A truth. The King's word never changes, but our experience of its truths never stops changing. In a sense, the book becomes what we think it's for. Violent zealots see it as a justification for their evil, and in their hands it becomes what they see.

"For you, indoctrinated by the lies of the Old City, the book is a Book of Duties. But for me, filled with the life of the New City, the book is a way to enjoy the King. A Book of Life. I see it more like the King intends people to see it, so that's how I experience it."

"Well, then I want to see what you see." Clint felt a fragile kind of hope flickering in his soul again. He snatched the book from Vita and stared hard at the cover. The Book of Duties. His heart sank. "I want to know the King. I want this book to be what he wants for me."

"Tell the King that."

"But he's not here. I've been looking for him for weeks."

"Humour me."

Clint sighed. "Fine. Okay. King, I want to know you, wherever you are. If I could see what Vita sees, that would be great." For a minute nothing happened. But then, as if waiting for him to stare at it, the cover became a thick liquid, swirling and morphing until the letters spelled *The Book of Life*.

Cracking it open excitedly, he flipped through a few dozen pages, skimming the words as they flew by. The words smelled like like Rosa's fresh bread, except they fed his soul instead of his stomach. The stories seemed to jump off the pages—or had he entered the book?

"Vita, where are all the lists? Are they all gone?" His heart was racing.

"Not all of them." Vita pointed to the page.
Clint read what Vita had highlighted. "'Love the King and love what he loves.' That's it? Just two things?"

"Actually, they're one thing. Loving the King means loving what and whom he loves. And you can spend your whole life doing that one thing. In fact, that's the point."

"I think I get it." Clint jumped up and down, then stopped, surprised at himself. He managed a breathless nod just before an unpredictable joy split the seams of his heart and tumbled out of his mouth as laughter.

"Clint, you're becoming a child again." Tears of joy welled up in Vita's blue eyes.

"What do you mean?"

"You can't enter Basileia with a grownup heart, friend. Nor can you experience true joy with an old heart, no matter how long you've lived here. Your joy tells me that your old heart is getting younger again. Your true self left the city without you knowing it, and now it is returning."

Clint spent the rest of the day pretty much inhaling The Book of Life. The next morning, he woke before the roosters and seriously considered finding one so he could scare the living feathers off it. He was tingling with excitement, ready to begin his daily readings and prayers. It was time to impress the King.

Unfortunately, the door screeched on its hinges on his way out and he was sure he had woken the entire household, maybe even the neighbours. He sat himself down on a mat just outside the door.

"So, I'm here, King. Please forgive me for my breakdown and everything I said about you and Basileia during my... uh, episode. Help me to seek you and to find you. Oh, and to get home to Monica and Sarah. Amen."

Clint opened his eyes and saw a tiny sparrow had landed on the welcome mat with him. Amused, he stretched out his hand. To his surprise, the bird hopped onto his hand and stood there flitting, bobbing its head, and looking into his eyes.

The door screeched again behind him. The sparrow flapped away, spooked by the loud noise. It was Shelah.

"What are you doing?" Shelah looked like she was still half asleep. Her hair was plastered to her face on one side.

"I'm doing my daily readings and prayers for the King. I want to be a good citizen."

Shelah blinked slowly, apparently still trying to wake up. She yawned. "That's an Old City thing, silly."

"What do you mean?"

"Devotional correctness, or whatever you call it. That's an Old City thing. We don't do that here."

"You don't do your daily readings and prayers?" He was shocked.

"Not like they do. Why should we?"

"Because that's what the King wants. That's what we need. Every good citizen ..."

"Does the Book of Life say that?"

"Sure it does!" Clint tried to stay calm. "Lots of times. Devotional correctness is what makes you a good citizen."

"Are you sure? That sounds a lot like the Book of Duties to me."

"How can you say that? The King wrote the book for us!"

"Yup. And I love it and read it all the time. It's so good! But there aren't any rules about reading it every day."

"No, it's in here. I'm positive." Clint gave his book a firm pat.

"Well, tell me when you find it." Shelah yawned again. "King, would you please show him the truth?" She stood there looking off into space for a second. "Oh, thank you. Then I'm going back to bed."

After Shelah went back inside, Clint's curiosity got the best of him. Scanning the book's index, he found nothing about devotional correctness or instructions for daily readings. An hour later the entire house was stirring and he still hadn't found a command or list or anything demanding a daily devotion time like he'd practiced in the Old City.

Next he searched the stories about the faith heroes and friends of the King. They were incredible warriors, lovers, poets, husbands, wives, and children—obviously favourites of the King's court—but none of them mentioned their daily devotions. They loved the King like crazy and talked to him often. They loved his book too. But they didn't seem to discipline themselves into a rigid daily routine—at least not like the one he'd malpracticed in the Old City. This discovery came as a huge relief.

"Breakfast, Clint." It was Rosa. He didn't have to be asked twice. Whatever the woman was cooking smelled delicious, and by this time he was ready to eat two breakfasts. After sitting down at the table he faced Shelah. Thankfully, she waited until after breakfast to ask him about his search.

"So?" Her eyes already knew the answer.

"I couldn't find it. But it must be there."

"What must be there?" Vita asked.

"Devotional correctness, daily readings. All the routines you people adopt to please the King so he can bless you."

Vita sighed. "Eat up. We've got a lot of work to do, Clint."

Clint inhaled breakfast and washed up. He followed his new mentor out the front door. Vita tried to lead him through the New City, but it was slow going since Clint felt compelled to stop and take in all the beautiful sights, smells, and sounds around him.

The shimmering glory of the air still astounded him. Every detail seemed to anoint him with energy and joy. Stopping to take a giant, slow breath, he cocked his head backward, lifting his hands toward the sky.

"Okay, this is officially awesome."

Chapter Nine:
Grace

Clint could hardly wait to see what the King had in store next. He and Vita were always up to something.

Dropping his gaze, Clint noticed the ground had changed under his feet since he had last looked at it. The pavement was solid and liquid at the same time, fluttering and rippling as he tested it with his feet.

"Let me guess, the ground is alive too."

Vita was already thirty paces ahead of him. The big man turned, feigning annoyance. "We really do have somewhere to go. You could work a little harder at keeping up. But in answer to your question, no, the ground is not alive."

"Then what's it made of?" Clint squatted on his haunches to touch it with his fingers. "It looks like cement—sort of—but it's not, is it? It's more like a giant touchscreen or something." The moment he made contact with the substance, shivers ran up and down his body and seemed to unite in his heart. It was almost impossible not to smile at the sensation.

"It's pure grace, Clint. Everywhere you go in Basileia, you're standing on the grace of the King. And you're smiling because of what grace is made of. Its very essence causes joy."

"I'll say." Clint's eyes brimmed with tears. It felt good to cry about something wonderful for a change. "So grace is basically a joy factory?"

"Yes. But if you think this is amazing, wait until you see where we're going." Vita gently took hold of his arm and led him through the rest of the city, to its very centre—a grassy hill with a lone cross on top.

"Clint, welcome to Golgotha."

Vita couldn't speak. Golgotha was the place where the King had given his life to pay for the sins of the citizens of Basileia and Kakos alike. Being there filled Clint with dread, wonder, and thankfulness all at once.

"Can I go up there?" Clint asked.

"Of course. I come back here as often as I can."

Up they went. Each step seemed holy. Every moment seemed to grow weightier and mightier than the one before it. Clint found himself looking down at the grass, which now looked more like a stream flowing down the hill.

In fact, it was a stream, a living fountain covering the entire hill, glazing it in the same grace that formed the foundation of the whole city. His eyes followed the water up to its source, slowly scaling the hill until he saw the cross standing before him.

He gasped.

The King was on it, bleeding and dying. Turning back to face Vita, he noticed that his friend's face was wet with tears. With great effort and a trembling chin, Vita spoke.

"No, the King isn't technically on the cross right now. But his sacrifice is eternal, which means every time we come to the cross, his blood still flows—as fresh as the day it was shed. In a sense, we all have to come to him, to look him in the eye at this place. Until we do that, we just can't know."

"Know what?"

"This is your journey, not mine."

Clint found himself trembling. The King was beaten badly and blood ran freely down his ragged flesh. Cruel spikes skewered his hands and feet, pinning him to the horrific wood. He writhed in pain.

"Who did this to him?" Anger smashed through Clint's veins.

Vita was sobbing loudly.

"Vita, who did this to him?"

The gentle giant turned to him. "I did."

But then another voice sounded, a voice so gentle it was powerful beyond words.

"You did too, Clint." The voice of the King. And there was no arguing with the King.

"I did?"

"Your sin had to be paid for," the King replied. "I had to make a way for you."

"I did this," Clint repeated, owning the thought, then hating himself.

"Clint, look at me."

"I can't. I feel terrible."

But the King was speaking to him. The King he had been searching for. The King he had rejected in the Old City. Trembling violently now, his eyes and nose flowed while shame and guilt wracked his body with physical pain. But Clint looked up. He met the King's gaze. Looked right into his eternal eyes.

They were Genesis, and they were Revelation. The sea and the stars. Sunrise and sunset, beginning and end. They were soaring joy and crushing sadness. Roaring thunder and gentle breeze. Fire and snow. And they were love. Pure, raging, unmaking, resurrecting, searing, scarring, dancing love—for him. Clint felt like he was being drawn into the King's soul. His eyes spun out a whirlpool of spirit and life.

"Now, Clint, give me your list." The King spoke again—but not from the cross. He now stood next to Clint, hand outstretched.

Clint didn't understand. "What list?"

"The one in your hand."

The one in his hand. How could he have missed it earlier? The damning, endless list of do's and don'ts, the thickening list of his endless failures, the list of duties and laws and rules he could never keep. The death of his passion. That list.

Clint gave the King the thick stack of paper in slow motion, as if in a trance. An massive burden rose from his soul a moment later and he wondered whether he weighed anything at all.

The beautiful trance was broken with a "Bang!" so loud that it rang in his ears. He nearly jumped out of his skin when he saw what the King was doing.

Bang!

He was nailing the accursed list to the cross.

Bang!

Pounding it with all his might, grunting with a fierce anger that nearly seemed unbecoming of the King. Almost.

Bang!

The list shrivelled right there on the cruel wood, flaking and rotting and flaming and shrinking—and then the crossbeam itself seemed to eat both the nail and then the list, sucking it right into the core.

It was gone. The ghastly list was gone. Now what?

CHAPTER TEN:

PRESENCE

Clint slept soundly that night, better than he had in weeks. He woke to find Shelah kneeling next to his mattress, her little face hovering just six inches from his own.

He groaned. "You got to sleep in yesterday. Go away."

"Look who's talking."

Clint stretched his arms above his head. "What time is it?"

"Time for lunch."

"Lunch?" He sat up with a start. "How long have I been out?"

"Just kidding." Shelah poked him in the ribs, bounding back from the bed like a rabbit. If she wanted a game, a game she would get. Clint erupted from the mattress, hands poised like claws with fingers wiggling.

"Are you... *ticklish*?"

She screamed in delight, scampering through the house with Clint close on her heels.

"Children, time to clean up for breakfast," Rosa called out sternly. She reached out to snag Clint's collar as he ran by. "That includes adults who haven't grown up," she scolded, one eyebrow raised in feigned disapproval.

"Hey, Vita said I had to become like a little child again, and I'm making excellent progress. Don't you think?"

"Childlike and childish are not the same thing. Wash up."

"Yes, Mother."

Clint grinned at her and she returned the smile. After washing up together in the metal basin and getting each other thoroughly wet, Clint and Shelah sat down together at the breakfast table, trying not to laugh. Breakfast was delicious, but with Vita around he didn't have much time to relish the moment.

"Let me guess, time for another walk?"

Clint was getting used to the walks. And loving them, actually. After Vita had kissed Rosa, Clint chased down Shelah to plant a peck on her cheek.

"Gross, boy germs!"

Clint laughed. "There's more where that came from."

The two men pushed through the screeching door and walked outside. Playing with Shelah made his heart throb with longing for his little Sarah. Only the King knew when—or if—he'd see her again.

"When can I connect with the King again, Vita?"

Vita's eyes sparkled again. "Today, Clint. Today."

They were just twenty paces from the house when Clint stopped in his tracks.

"What now?" Vita teased, pretending to be disgusted.

Something had been nagging at Clint through his dreams during the night. Vita had led him to Golgotha the previous afternoon. Right in the middle of the city. Which made no sense—Basileia was built onto a mountain.

"Where is it? Where is the mountain? And the Old City? And all the levels?"

"There are no levels in Basileia."

"Very funny. I climbed them. I lived on them. I even fell from one."

"An Old City illusion, Clint. A deception devised to make the privileged few feel self-righteous. The ground is level in the New City. There is no climb, no ascending to the King. He lives among us. And when you come to fully live here, the Old City loses its appeal. Soon after that, it vanishes entirely."

"Then why do I still have a bruise on my elbow?"

"The Old City is a vapour, but the pain it causes is very real. Living here will heal that soon enough."

"Yeah, the New City is pretty great. But I have to say, I sure miss the apples."

Vita scrunched up his face. "Pardon me?"

"The apples. I pretty much lived on them in the Old City."

"Ah, Nomothesia." Vita shook his head.

"You know her?"

"Sure I know her."

"Her apples are delicious, aren't they? And they made me hungry for the book."

"Did she ever tell you where she got them?"

"I never thought to ask."

"Every morning she leaves Basileia to collect them outside the gates."

"Outside?"

"Come, I'll show you." He started walking again, and as usual, Clint was taking his time.

"Today, Clint." He waved his companion forward. Clint followed, still gawking at the shimmering world around him, chuckling at the grace lining the streets. Fifteen minutes later they were approaching the city gate.

"I don't want to leave," he said. "I mean, I want to go home, to see my family. But I like it here. A lot."

"We aren't leaving. Trust me."

Toothless Joe cowered behind the cart as they approached, but Clint extended his hand. "Sorry about the other day, bud."

Looking first to Vita for reassurance, he took Clint's hand and shook it. "That's okay. Old City or New City?"

Clint laughed. "New City, definitely." The man held out a book. A Book of Life.

"No, I'm good, thanks. Mine transmogrified itself."

Pulling Clint by the arm, Vita stepped through the gate. He pointed to a rough spot on the gravel just outside. "That's where I found you the other day."

Clint smiled. He had come a long way, hadn't he? Directly to their right stood the bridge.

"Here we are."

Clint stood looking out over the chasm. "What am I supposed to be looking at, exactly?"

"First of all, that big tree over there, beside the bridge. That's where your friend gets her apples."

"Yeah, I saw it on my way in."

The thing's trunk was thicker than a monster truck. It's crown was immense. Stepping closer, he saw that it was peppered with the apples he'd lived on the past few weeks. Some of the branches were so full of fruit they had bent over until they were resting on the ground.

"Oh, man. Can I pick some? I've got a craving."

"If you'd like."

Clint walked up to the tree and paused there, standing in its shadow. He was about to pluck a big apple when he was startled by a rustling above him. Before he could react, a bright green snake with barbed fangs dropped its head from the foliage. Clint jumped back.

"Whoah!"

"It's the Tree of Knowledge, friend."

"The what?"

"Remember in the book of Genesis? The tree of Knowledge in the garden of Eden?"

"Yeah. And you're saying this is that tree?"

"It is."

"But didn't God remove it from the Garden back back when Adam and Eve were banished?" He was now standing next to Vita several paces back from the Tree.

"No, Clint. He transplanted the Tree of Life in Basileia, but the Tree of Knowledge just adapted, splitting off into a thousand different forms, sending its greedy roots into every nook and cranny of the earth."

"So the apples are bad, then?"

"True knowledge comes from friendship with the King. It is not just for the mind, but the heart. Even the Book of Life isn't an end in itself. It is designed to lead us past itself to him."

"That's deep. But isn't Nomothesia worried about the snake? What if it bites her?"

"She's already been bitten, Clint. But enough of that. Take a look at the bridge." Clint looked.

"It's impressive, that's for sure."

"Keep looking. Does it look familiar to you?"

"Well, not ..." Clint began, then stopped. He looked at the bridge again. The span, the spire, the supporting pillar just beneath it. Then it struck him. He gasped. "It's a giant cross!"

"Not a cross. *The* cross. And what's it doing?"

"Uh, bridging?"

"Yes. Between Kakos and Basileia. Between the old life and the King."

"Which is how I got here. I get that."

"But where is here?" Vita's eyes flashed with passion. Clint didn't grasp his line of thought, and Vita saw it. "In the Old City you spent every waking hour engaged in the Pursuit. Why?"

"Because the King wants us to seek him. Because I wanted to get closer to him. To find him. So I could get back home."

"And?"

Clint felt his eyes mist over, then fill with tears. "I got a few notes and found a footprint here and there. But that was all. It was so frustrating."

"It nearly killed Rosa too. I found her collapsed outside the gate years ago, very close to the spot where I found you. That was ten years ago, before we married."

"She's a beautiful woman, Vita. You're a lucky man."

"Do you know why she's so beautiful?"

Clint shook his head.

"Because she's living in the secret I'm about to show you." Clint desperately wanted what Rosa had. She reminded him of his Monica.

Vita turned to stand face to face with him and gripped his shoulders tightly. "Listen very closely."

"Okay."

"Clint, you will never get closer to the King."

Clint's heart sank. But he knew it was true. His lip quivered with emotion. He would never get back home, would he? His hope was all but gone.

"I'm sure you sense the truth by now: All the hide and seek of the Old City is futile. There is nothing a mortal can ever do to ascend into the King's presence, nothing any of us can do to bridge this chasm."

The telltale twinkle flashed in the man's eye again. Clint just stood there, numb. His brain wasn't following yet.

"Clint, there is nothing any mortal can do. But the King can draw near to us. The King can bridge the chasm. And as you can see, he's already done it."

Clint furrowed his brow. "That's it? That's your secret?"

"Yes."

"I already know that. You're talking about how I was delivered from Kakos. But once we're here in the city, it's different. All good citizens have to get into the Pursuit."

"The Pursuit is real, but you have it backwards."

"Backwards?"

"The King is pursuing us, Clint."

"What?"

"Think about it. He bridged the chasm to bring us near. To bring himself near. So we never have to seek him again."

Never seek the King? Clint felt something in his heart shift. A kernel of faith sprang into existence as they stepped out onto the bridge.

"He's given himself to us, Clint. Fully and forever."

Another kernel of faith popped. His vision began to swirl.

"He's right there above you. Look."

Clint nearly choked on his surprise. The King was hovering there above him, filling the sky with his splendour.

"He's in front of you, Clint."

And there he was, majestic and smiling broadly. Right in front of him.

"And all around you."

He truly was. Everywhere, all around him.

"And behind you."

Clint was about to spin around to look when he felt a strong hand rest on his shoulder from behind. A hand graced with a royal ring. A hand scarred through the palm. Clint bit his lip as giant tears spilled down his cheeks. Vita stepped back, nodded reverently at the King, and walked cheerfully toward home.

"Vita is a true brother," the King said. "But now you know I am with you."

Clint's legs failed him and he crumpled into a spasmodic joy. The grace on the bridge rippled as he fell.

"Look, I'm even beneath you." Those last words rumbled like thunder, shaking Clint to the core. He looked down and saw the King there too, smiling at him from within the bridge, filling it, holding him up.

In fact, the King was the bridge.

Just when he thought he might explode with wonder, the King above him, around him, in front of him, behind him, and beneath him multiplied somehow, the originals remaining exactly as they were but part of them moving toward him like rainbows of life. And then they charged inside his body, melting into his frame, becoming one with his spirit. His body snapped rigid, full of power and glory. Clint was sure his eyes were on fire, though he felt no pain.

"Clint, my son, because you put your faith in me and what I did on the cross, I am in you, and you are in me, and I am in my Father." The words came from the King's heart, and they felt like a thunderclap. The sound pushed deep cracks through many of the Old City lies within him. He could sense them buckling under the explosive strain of the King's presence, finally shattering into a million pieces and evaporating.

"Don't seek me, Clint," the King said, whispering now. "Never again. You already have me. Don't pursue me; enjoy me. Don't chase after me; let me catch you. From this moment, let my presence transcend both faith and feelings. Let this truth become a deep knowing that never wavers no matter what happens around you."

"Okay. Wow. So I..."

Clint slipped into a prostrate position there on the bridge, lying flat on his face for a very long time. The sensation of the King's indwelling was so intense he could hardly stand it.

"I'll never seek you again," he said, weeping. "Never. Thank you, thank you, thank you."

The King's own heartbeat was throbbing in Clint's chest, pounding with joy. Incredibly, he sensed that the King was as happy as he was. Maybe more. He lay there all day watching the sun complete its course across the sky.

Chapter Eleven:
Quenched

Vita let Clint catch up with his soul the next morning. "Take it slow, friend. There's only so much transformation a person can take."

Even so, Clint was itching to explore the New City. Later in the morning he decided to take a walk on his own. The King thought it was a fantastic idea.

"May I come along?"

Clint chuckled. "You're sort of everywhere."

"Ah, you're catching on. But you can go anywhere without noticing me. You can shut me out."

"And I used to be a pro at that. But not anymore. I love this new way, where I can talk to you any time I want."

"And I can talk to you any time I want. I dwell in every soul that makes me King, but most people don't realize it and go their whole lives without acknowledging my presence within them."

"They waste their time on the Pursuit?"

"Exactly, Clint. Why spend your time seeking something you already have?"

Clint felt a pang of loneliness. The King read his expression. "You miss your family."

Tears welled up in his eyes. "I've been trying to find a way back home for weeks now. I got so excited about your presence on the bridge yesterday that I forgot to ask you about that."

"That was why you sought me. Why you memorized scripture. Why you drank so much water from the spring."

Clint nodded, ashamed. The King knew everything. "I'm so sorry. I just wanted to go home."

The King strode up to him and clasped his shoulders with his regal hands. "I won't allow myself to be used, Clint."

At those words the tears spilled from Clint's eyes onto his cheeks, running down until they collected on the tip of his chin. The King gently reached out and wiped them away.

"Do you still want to go home?"

Clint nodded. "More than anything. Well, almost anything."

"I can send you back right now if you'd like. But I must tell you, I'm not finished with you here. It would sadden me to let you go. But the choice is yours. It's always yours."

Clint felt ill. He had just been given the freedom to choose his family on one hand and the King on the other. Standing there in front of him, knees knocking together and blood draining from his face, he suddenly felt nauseous. He collapsed at the King's feet, clutching the golden sandals with desperate hands.

"Don't do this to me. It's not fair." His tears were soaking the King's feet. Glancing up at the King's face, he saw the unyielding truth. He wanted to be chosen above everyone and everything, even above his girls. There was no way around it. The King would honour Clint's choice, but he would not back down from the invitation.

"Then ... I'm going to need to think about it."

"I will come by first thing tomorrow."

Clint tossed and turned that night, dizzied by the tension he felt in his soul. Hour after hour his thoughts spun in vicious circles. The decision was too difficult. How could he live without Monica and Sarah? He couldn't bear to think of losing them. How could the King be so cruel? It felt like choosing between life and death, but in this case both paths meant the death of something painfully precious.

After hours of agonizing, one simple thought seemed to settle amidst the maelstrom of confusion: Monica would never want him to choose her over the King. Never. Clint groaned in agony with that realization. He pounded the grace lining the wall next to his cot. There was only one right thing to do, and he hated it with every fibre in his being. Worse, he hated himself for hating it. Trembling with fear, he heard himself speak the awful words.

"I ... suppose I'll stay."

"I didn't ask what you suppose." The King's voice was tender but firm.

A moment later Clint found himself lying flat on his stomach on the brink of the chasm between Kakos and Basileia. Both of his arms were pulled taut over the edge, straining to hold onto something. He was horrified to realize that in one hand he gripped Monica, and in the other, his little Sarah. Both of his girls dangled over the dark abyss, held fast only by his stubborn will.

He was shocked to find that their eyes were not brimming with fear, but with tranquility.

"Let us go, sweetheart."

Clint's heartbeat nearly cracked his own ribs at the thought. "No way, Monica. Never." Clint gritted his teeth as his rigid body slipped an inch forward toward the chasm. His arms burned with the strain.

"Trust me, Clint." The King was with him, hand on his shoulder.

"I can't let them go. I can't." He had to save them, not let them go. Pulling with all his might, screaming with frustration, he found he couldn't move them an inch, never mind back up over the edge. His panic became a boiling rage. He slipped another few inches forward. "I'll never let go, girls. Never." He tried to dig his feet into the grass, but couldn't find anything to stop his sliding.

"Daddy, it's okay. The King will save us." Her eyes shone with faith.

"Sarah…"

"Trust me, Clint."

Oh, he wanted to. He wanted to trust the King more than anything.

He turned to look into the King's face, now wet with tears like his. "Help me. I can't pull them up, but I can't let them go."

"I am helping you. Trust me."

His eyes locked with the King's again, and something wondrous and terrifying passed between them. In a moment too awful to describe, the King's words suddenly jumped to life within him. They just clicked. And with the faith came peace. He turned to face the girls. Their eyes were still clear, full of the same stillness he now felt. Everything seemed to slow down — his heartbeat, his breathing, his mind.

"Honey, I have to let you go."

Monica smiled. "I know."

He let go.

Clint awoke from the dream drenched with sweat. The King stood at his bedside. And now he wasn't just the King, but in a deeper way than ever before, *his* King. The giant monarch said nothing at first, but offered Clint his hand and lifted him to his feet. As soon as they were standing together, he embraced Clint heartily, nearly crushing him with his kingly strength. Clint closed his eyes again, drinking in the affection. He felt the King kiss his forehead.

"Thank you, Clint. Whoever loses their life will find it."

He felt the King relax his grip and let go of the hug. When Clint opened his eyes he saw him standing back, rubbing his hands together with great relish.

"Now, why go hungry and thirsty when you can be satisfied?"

Clint shook his head, trying to switch gears after what had just happened. Truth be told, he felt like he'd just been hit by a bus.

Rosa stepped into the conversation. "I beg your pardon, but I see where this is going. Could you please take this outside?"

"No, no, do it inside. It'll be fun!" Shelah stood nearby as well. She clapped her hands with glee. Rosa shot her a look.

"Do what?" Clint looked to his friends to clarify, but they ignored him.

"He's the King, Rosa. If he wants to do it inside, let him do it." Vita smiled broadly.

"Of course I'll let him do it, Vita. I'm just asking. There's no harm in asking. Why make a mess if we can do it outside?"

The King strode over to Rosa, robes flowing behind him. He took her face in his hands and then bent over to kiss her on the cheek. "If you would prefer we take it outside, we'll take it outside."

"Yes, thank you."

"You're welcome. This time, at least."

"What? What are you talking about?" Clint realized he was shouting because everyone turned to look at him. He was embarrassed but held their gaze. "What?"

"Take it outside," they said, bursting into raucous laughter. The King took Shelah by the hand. "Would you like to help me, my love?"

"Help you? Oh, yes!" She jumped up and down like a pogo stick. "I'll help. I'll help."

The moment the King let her go she bolted across the room and clamped onto Clint. "Come with me," she said, giggling again. Clint was still bewildered, but let her yank him out the screeching door before he could protest. The King followed her until she had led them about twenty feet away from the house.

"Here. Yup. We'll do it right here."

The King smiled broadly. "Well done, Shelah. Now Clint, I have something to give you. Or rather, I've already given it to you, but you don't realize it yet. And as you've already seen, most of my gifts don't become real to you until you realize they are."

Clint nodded. He couldn't imagine what the King might still have in store. He just stood there a moment, stately and silent. Incredibly, so did Shelah.

"Do you thirst for me, Clint?"

"Yeah." A lump rose in his throat. "More than anything."

"Would you like me to give you a drink?"

"A real drink, not like the fountain of death in the Old City? A drink like the ones you left for me on the table in my old house?"

"Better," the King answered. "The best drink I could give you there was like a handful of sand compared to what I can give you here."

"Well, then want it." Clint clenched his fists. "I need it."

"Then Shelah will show you the fountain. A fountain that never stops flowing. A fountain that you can come to any time you want. A fountain of life, the water of my Spirit. Would you like to drink in my Spirit, Clint?"

"Drink… your spirit?"

"Trust me, Clint, you want this." Shelah's eyes shone brightly.

Clint nodded, then began to tremble, as though the deepest parts of him were coming undone. His teeth started chattering. His knees knocked together. "You would share that with me? Your Spirit?"

"I hold nothing back." The King winked at Shelah.

"Now?" she asked.

"Yes, princess. Now. Show him the spring."

Biting her lip, Shelah tried to keep a straight face. She turned and walked right up to Clint. She inched closer until she was standing six inches from him, her little heart beating like a drum. He could hear her excited breathing.

"The spring. The spring."

"Yes?"

"The spring is ... right ... here." And with that, she reached up, standing on her tippy-toes, and planted her little palm in the middle of his chest.

Clint stumbled back. Something rumbled within him. Shelah was laughing again, spinning and jumping in circles.

"The spring, the spring, it makes me sing," she shouted. The King began to dance with her, but the next moment everything became a blur.

A floodgate had opened inside him. From the very pit of his emptiness, from the hollow of hollows within him, sprang a torrent of fresh, cool water.

"What ..." His question was cut short as the water explurted like a geyser from his mouth, from his fingertips, out of his toes, chest, and even from the top of his head. He danced madly in circles as the water sloshed everywhere, soaking the King, dousing Shelah, and even spraying through the window to spatter Rosa. A special touch from the King.

"Keep it outside." Rosa laughed heartily and a moment later she and Vita had joined the water party. Water was flowing out of all of them, forming a bubbling pool of delicious refreshment on the stones around the dwelling.

A few moments later the flow decreased some, enough for him to be able to talk properly again. "I love... it." Clint jumped up and down with Shelah. "I love you, King. You're... you're... you're life itself."

The King's eyes were brimming with childlike wonder and love. "Now, then, let's check."

"Check what?"

"Are you thirsty for me, Clint?"

Clint stopped short, soaking wet and speechless. The whole family paused in silence, marking the moment with a holy reverence.

"Thirsty? I ... well ... no."

"A little thirsty, maybe?"

"No. Not at all, actually."

"Somewhere deep down?"

"No. I'm totally satisfied. In fact, I can't imagine ever being thirsty again."

Vita grinned. "How could you be, if the spring of his Spirit is flowing from within you?"

"That's it exactly," Clint agreed.

"You're finally getting it," the King replied, laughing. "Clint, you have spent too much of your life trying to fill the void in your soul."

"And now you just filled it for me. So awesome."

"Actually, I filled it the moment you stepped across the bridge into Basileia. But the Old City kept that blessing hidden from you by telling you to search for it. With the spring of living water within you you won't have to fill yourself up with anything, because you're already one with me. Just accept this as your new reality."

"Will it always flow like this? This powerful, this satisfying?"

"Always," Vita said, putting his arm around him.

"But it won't always be so visible or emotional," the King said. "And there will be special times when I pour out even more of my Spirit on you. Or rather, you will experience more."

"Thank goodness it's not always this messy." Rosa was already sweeping the wet stones, pushing the water down a drain.

"What's wrong with messy? Some of my best work is messy," the King said.

"I'll say." Clint sighed. And for the first time since crossing the bridge, he felt complete.

Chapter Twelve:
Rhythm

Over the next few weeks Clint spent nearly every day with the King. He often asked him questions, thanked him for the new life and the New City, and poured out his heart in worship and gratitude.

In turn, the King answered many questions about the new life and the New City. Then again, his answers always raised more questions, but exploring the truth was more invigorating then he'd ever known before.

Vita and Rosa often joined them, along with many friends and neighbours. Clint loved the deep sense of community that emerged so naturally from their common bond with the King. Today, however, he and the King were alone—which was good, because Clint had another question for him.

"So I've been thinking. You crucified the list, right?"

"Yes."

"And ended the Pursuit by pursuing us."

"Yes."

"And quenched my thirst. Which was totally epic, by the way."

"Thank you."

"Right. But now I'm not sure how to follow you. Or even what to do with myself. In the Old City it was like A plus B equals C. Do this to get that. It was clear."

"And dead."

"Yeah, and dead. And believe you me, I don't want to go back. But what now? Those old city routines are all I know."

"Routines are the Old City counterfeit for a life of rhythm."

"Meaning?"

"Every day with me will be different, and should be. We have a relationship now. A friendship."

"Yeah. And I love it."

"And what would happen to our friendship if we did the same things in the same order at the same time in the same place every single day, forever? What if we made it a routine? A discipline? An expectation? What if we spent each day trying to recapture what we did the day before?"

"That would get stale pretty quick."

"Exactly." Taking Clint's hand, the King led him to a curious window set into a wall to their left. "Look here." His eyes were twinkling like Vita's, or was it the other way around? Either way, Clint obeyed. He strode over to the window and peered inside. Before him lay a large garden. The flowers and foliage were bursting with life. It was magnificent.

"Hey, I've never seen this garden here before. Or the window, for that matter."

The King smiled. Clint loved it when he smiled.

"*Were* they here before?" Clint asked.

"No, they weren't. And both the window and the garden will be gone tomorrow, like many of the moments I give you."

"But this is great. I want to come back here."

"I know you do. So many people stumble onto a precious moment with me and try to reproduce it by doing the same things over and over again. It's like they believe it was what they did that created the moment. A plus B equals C."

The King sighed. "To be honest, they aren't the only ones that get tired of those games. I'm much more original than that, and I want to be original with you. Windows open, close, and even disappear. Every one of my sunsets is unique. No moment is ever repeated. Every blade of grass, every snowflake, every sunrise, every storm, everything I create is given a magic all its own."

"What does that mean for me?"

"If you let me guide you, I'll lead you through a lifetime of special moments. They will seem mostly random to you, but they're anything but. Every one of them is part of my strategic plan."

"Okay… "

"Sometimes I will lie you down in green pastures. Sometimes the path will meander next to still waters. Every day's journey opens up a different section of trail with unique challenges and blessings, for my sake as much as yours.

"Some days are dark, and will move us through pain and even death. But we'll always be together. I'll be continuously blessing you, making your spring overflow. Wherever you are, you'll be leaving a glistening trail of goodness and love behind you like a path of clues for others to find so they can enter my life too. Like Vita and Rosa did for you. And through it all, you'll be alive in my presence and I will be in yours."

Clint shook his head. "Wow. That's so different from what I'm used to. I was taught 'practice makes perfect' or something like that. But that was our idea more than yours, wasn't it?"

"Yes. When you take the initiative, you've got your agenda to fulfill, which is why you've often been disappointed with the results. But every encounter I initiate with you is a divine encounter. Has one day been alike since you came to the New City?"

Clint laughed. "Not even close."

"Well, that will continue if you walk with me. Quite often I'll open the Book of Life and read to you and it will literally jump to life in your hands. Other times we'll just talk as we are now. Sometimes we'll walk, sometimes we'll share a meal, or watch my creatures at play. We'll regularly venture into Kakos to show people the way of life or spend the day helping others."

"Okay, but don't I need my routines to stay on track?"

"On track with what? Your sense of accomplishment? The list I crucified? What are you measuring, Clint?"

"I'm not sure anymore."

"Well, how about how much time you spend studying my word each day? How many verses you memorize? What people think of you? Drop the the math of pride. Just walk with me. I will guide you through special seasons of focus designed to grow your faith as I see fit."

"So there will still be a structure of sorts?"

"Of course, but my structures are built on rhythms, not routines. Think of night and day, the changing seasons, your heartbeat, your breathing, and the growth of your soul. Clint, your spiritual development isn't up to you. Self-discipline does not produce passion; passion produces self-discipline."

He put his hands on Clint's shoulders and looked at him longingly. His gaze held an earnest sadness that broke Clint's heart.

"Did I do something wrong?"

"I'm real, Clint."

"I know that now."

"Then treat me that way. Let me grow you. I will always give you what you need when you need it. Don't live as if I don't exist. Don't walk through life like I have no interest in guiding you. Live and move within me every day. Be completely open to what I want in every moment."

"I can do that," Clint said, nodding.

"No you can't. But that's all right. I don't need perfection from you. And you'll improve over time."

"I'll do my best, then."

"No you won't. At least, not always. But I'll work with what you give me. By the way, did you enjoy the sparrow?"

Clint smiled. "The one that landed on my knee?"

"I told him to find you. To share my smile with you. Think of him as a love note from my heart to yours."

"Thank you."

Clint paused, trying to find words for his next question. "Why do people live in the Old City at all? Why the Book of Duties, why the list, why the guilt, the Pursuit, the hungering, thirsting, pining, and fighting? I don't get it."

For the first time since he had met the King, Clint noticed a tear well up in his eyes and trickle down his great cheek. "There are many reasons, and all of them break my heart. People don't want to give me control. They try to use me, as you did. They want power for themselves. It makes them feel righteous and significant to check things off a list, even if it's the wrong one. That way they can measure their growth against what other people are doing. They substitute their own work for the work I've already done for them. They focus on what makes them feel good about themselves. What makes them look more spiritual."

"Instead of what makes you happy."

"Exactly. Structure seems safer, more predictable, more controllable. When it comes to faith, most choose dutiful routine over passionate relationship. But as you can see now, the power in our relationship lies in its flux, not in its structure. Structure kills the power of surprise, which is one of my favourite tools."

The King suddenly stopped, and took Clint's elbow in his hands. "Look."

Clint looked. A young boy was tottering along a high fence, balancing as best he could. But not well enough.

"Boys will be boys."

Without warning, the boy lost his footing and fell headlong from the fence, smacking the back of his skull on the cobblestone street. Clint gasped.

The King was already beside the young lad. "Come here, Clint."

Clint obeyed. "Is he breathing? I can't see him breathing. We have to help him."

"I am helping him. Come closer."

Clint obeyed again.

"Put your hand on the back of his head." Again Clint obeyed, and nearly recoiled in shock at the swelling mass he felt growing there.

"Aw, man. This isn't good."

"Tell him to wake up. In my name."

"But—!"

"It's okay. Just do it."

Clint did as he was told. "Wake up. In the name of the King." Clint could hardly think, and fearful tears rimmed his eyes. He glanced up at the King, who didn't look worried at all.

A moment later Clint's heart fluttered as the awful swelling melted away like butter on a skillet. And then the little boy woke up, flailing and gasping for air. Clint stepped back, shocked beyond words.

The boy jumped to his feet and skittered down the street, apparently none the worse for wear.

"How ... how did I do that?"

"You didn't. I did it through you."

"But ..."

The King laughed. "But what?"

"I didn't pray."

"No, you didn't."

"But don't I have to pray and fast for things like that to happen? In the Old City ..."

The King smiled. "Clint, miracles don't come from prayer. They come from cooperating with my Spirit."

"I don't get it."

"And yet you just did it. Faith is a conversation of obedience that takes many forms. Many times faith becomes prayer. But just as often it manifests as a hug, a meal, a shoulder to cry on, a healing moment, or even a courageous stand for justice. If you pray when I want you to act, that prayer is useless. If you act when I want you to pray, you're acting in your own strength."

"But ..."

"Enough buts, Clint. You can do anything if you listen to my voice and do what I tell you. That's one of the most important lessons of the kingdom. And it's also why no two days with me are alike. My Spirit is like the wind blowing free. If you listen to me, you'll be like the wind too."

"Okay. But if every day is different, how do I make sure I balance all the things I'm supposed to be doing?"

"You don't." That stopped Clint in his tracks.

"I don't?"

"Balancing all those things is my job."

"I guess so."

"Clint, trust me on this. If you walk with me, you'll never lack anything. Ever. And I've never asked you to be balanced. At least, not when it comes to our relationship."

"Say what?"

"I've never asked you to be balanced. I want you to be passionate. To be wholly mine, to love me. And passion is one of the most unbalanced forces in the universe. That's why I love it. Many things just can't get done within the prison of balance.

"When balance and routine become too important, you begin to serve them instead of me. Without being rescued by passion, love eventually withers under the staleness of duty. Which is why you almost died there in the Old City. You had buried yourself under the thick sediment of an empty way of life I never asked you to embrace. That, my friend, was what you call an epic fail."

"You got that right." Clint reflected on his failures. "I guess I didn't know any better back then."

"But you do now."

Clint nodded. But out of nowhere, a wave of homesickness found him. "Please don't be insulted by my asking, but am I ever going to get back home?"

"You're already home."

"No, I mean my real home."

The King smiled, raising an eyebrow. He was about to say something, but stopped himself. Clint dropped the question for the time being.

What a day.

Chapter Thirteen:

VICT⊕RY

Several weeks into his life in the New City, Clint was already learning to live out the powerful rhythms of spiritual passion. He enjoyed drinking in the glory of the kingdom. He found his footing on the foundation of grace, and it helped him walk with the King, talk with the King, and listen to the King. Over time, this intimacy felt like the most natural thing in the world.

Staying with Vita, Rosa, and Shelah was wonderful too. He felt like he was part of a rich extended family including the community around their home. They had their moments, but with grace flowing everywhere, conflicts seemed so much easier to resolve. Doing life with others was a new thing for Clint, but soon he could hardly imagine going without it. And them.

Once a week he joined the throng of other Basileians who gathered at the temple, but it was nothing like the lukewarm cloisterings of the Old City dwellers. This was a fellowship of satisfied souls enjoying encouragement and camaraderie, a real and ongoing celebration of the King's grace and presence.

It felt wonderful to worship with the King sitting right there, present in all his glory. Clint's love for him grew deeper with every passing day. He missed his family, but he'd made his choice. He would follow the King wherever the path led him.

One day the King found Clint reclining with Vita and his friends as they studied the Book of Life together in the park.

"I'm here for Clint."

Clint looked at Vita. Vita smiled.

"Go, my friend. When the King comes for you, you don't hesitate." Clint got up and followed the King. It struck him he rarely knew where he was going anymore. But it didn't matter, because he knew who he was following.

"I have a very special place to show you today." The King's face was full of pride again. Whenever the King had that look, something amazing was about to happen.

"Where is it?" Clint laughed. "Let me guess. It's within me, right?"

The King laughed with him. "No, not within you. But always with you. Turn around."

Clint turned. Standing tall before him was a magnificent building encircled by high archways. Its most curious feature was the absence of doors of any kind. The whole structure was open from every side and had seemingly appeared out of thin air.

"Cool. What is it?"

"My royal treasury."

Inside the building were countless piles of shimmering treasures, a buffet of wealth and wonder beyond Clint's wildest imaginings. A dozen trees laden with astounding fruit ringed the outer fringes of the room. He had never seen such riches. People were coming and going through the gates in a constant stream. Those who were leaving were carrying out fruit and treasures by the sackful.

"Treasury, huh? That's an understatement."

"No, not an understatement. It's just that human language can't contain it's grandeur."

"What are those people carrying?" Clint asked.

"Blessings. The riches in glory I share with you. Everything you see here is yours to enjoy. Every need you have in life has a blessing to match it in my treasury, and it is my joy to give you every one of them—if I haven't given them already."

"Don't people abuse that? I mean, don't they take more than they need or steal other people's blessings?"

"If you delight in me, I will shape your desires, Clint. And besides, none of the blessings you see there belong to others."

Clint's eyes widened. "All that is mine?"

"All of it. But not all at once. Leave the timing to me."

"And all I have to do is ask?"

"Sometimes you have to ask. But not always. Mostly you just have to trust me."

"What do you mean?"

"What kind of King and Father would I be if I only gave you what you needed when you asked for it? I don't share my treasures with you because you ask. I share them because I love you."

"In the Old City they told me to claim things. To remind you about what you promised and insist on it until I got what I asked for."

The King sighed. "In the Old City, they don't really pray, they pray-monger. It hurts me more than you know. Trust my heart, Clint. My treasury is always only full of blessings fit for the child who needs them."

Clint had to ponder that. "So when any of us come, it only holds our own blessings?"

"Yes. Unless of course you come to get something to share. Which will happen pretty much every day."

"And it's always there for all of us, individually, all at the same time?" Clint's head was spinning.

"I have blessed you with every spiritual blessing here in the heavenly realm, Clint."

Clint sat down, totally overwhelmed. "Is that where I am? In the heavenly realm?"

"You are in two places. I have made you a spiritual being with a physical body. Your body walks the earth while your spirit traverses Basileia. All my blessings are here, waiting for you to find them and use them in the physical realm. I've given you faith as the river through which the riches of this realm can flow into the other."

Clint's pulse was racing. "I'm in two places at once?"

The King nodded and put his hand on Clint's shoulder. "And today, we will visit Kakos."

"Can Vita come?"

"He's already there."

Clint felt his pulse quicken. "Then we have to go and help him. The diabolon will eat him alive."

"We're there too, Clint."

He looked around, his eyes darting down at the ground, at the swirling gold-dusted air, then back at the King. "I don't understand."

"Which is why you do not see."

"Then... help me see."

"Clint, that's a great prayer." The King reached out and touched Clint's eyes. "Now look up."

Clint looked up. He gasped at the sight. All around him the New City still stood, shining and majestic—but the space was shared by dark buildings, pillars of rank smoke, and soaring diabolon.

"An invasion?" Turning to the King, he tugged at his shoulder. "Quick. I need my armour."

The King didn't move.

"Clint, I am your armour. I am the salvation that guards your mind. I am the righteousness that protects your heart. I am the truth that keeps your spiritual balance. I am the readiness that prepares you for anything Kakos can throw at you. I give you the words that cut the enemy to pieces. Believing these things will become your shield against whatever the enemy tries to do to you. Do you believe me?"

The fire in the King's eyes was enough for Clint. "Yes. I believe you."

"Then you are already dressed in armour fit for a King." And he really was—outfitted with armour so marvellous, he felt sheepish even wearing it. He bowed to the King.

"And as for the diabolon, they are not invading anything. This is their home ground, for now at least."

"No, that can't be. This is Basileia." Clint's tension was rising because of the circling monsters, now roaring loudly as they flapped their reptilian wings through the streets of the city.

"Clint, my New City is established right in the midst of Kakos."

"But the bridge? The cross?"

"They're real. My sacrifice is the bridge a person must cross between cities. But Kakos and Basileia are also spiritual cities overlaying both each other and the physical world. I'll show you more of this later. For now, let me show you how to deal with these enemies."

"Sure. Okay. I'll fight them if you want me to," Clint said, trembling with fear but enflamed with loyalty for the King.

But the King had vanished. He was nowhere to be seen. And just as suddenly, one of the circling diabolon landed on the cobbled stone just ahead of him with a meaty thud. Clint gripped his sword with fear.

"I know you," the monster said. "I knocked you from the wall in the Old City and left you for dead, didn't I? You snivelling, impotent coward. You're going to wish I had killed you that day."

The muscled beast's growl resonated deeply in its barrelled chest and its ivory mane prickled with rage. Poisonous saliva dripped from its jaws.

Terror tingled up Clint's spine. "Your majesty, come back. Help me."

The King appeared again, seemingly out of thin air. He ignored the diabolos. "Clint, I never left."

"I couldn't see you." Clint quailed with fear.

"Like now, you mean?" The King vanished again. "See? You can still hear me. That's because I'm right here. Now do as I say."

As the King spoke the diabolos lowered its head and stepped forward, opening its jaws wider than Clint thought possible. Blood and hate spewed from it's gaping mouth. "I'm going to devour you, Old City dweller. You faithless, foolish failure!"

It was true. He was a failure. Just like the knight killed beside him in the Old City. But he didn't want to die. Clint's arms felt useless and his sword dragged him down, like an anvil in his hands. It was too heavy for him. Without help, he would certainly perish.

"My Lord and King, I beg you. Show me how to fight."

"You don't have to fight."

The King's words were forming in his mind now. They were every bit as clear as they had been when the King had been standing right next to him. In fact, they sounded exactly the same as the audible voice had.

The King read his thoughts. "Remember: I have defeated the creature before you. They are subject to me. And I am within you. Which means…"

"They're subject to me too," Clint said, finishing the King's thought. The monster froze for a moment, a wave of fear rippling its way across the feral face. Then it took a step forward, howling like a red-hot kettle.

Clint inhaled confidence from his invisible King. The thing took another step closer. Now its savage face was just inches from his own. He could smell its sulphuric breath as it opened its mouth wide again, exposing a tight mouthful of broken daggers. It trembled with bloodlust.

"I have nothing to fear from you."

"Just use my name," the King spoke into his mind. "Like you did with the injured boy. It's time to lay down the law." At those words, Clint felt courage and righteous anger surge through him, almost like he'd been plugged into a powerful current of electricity.

"I am a servant son of the King of kings." Clint's chest swelled with power.

"You don't have to raise your voice," the King said.

"Sorry." Clint looked the diabolos straight in the eyes. "Okay, so in the name of the King, step down."

"I am a free choosing being like you are. I can disobey you if I like." The beast snarled again, but Clint noticed its rage melting under a mounting fear.

"Take that up with the King."

The diabolos blinked, confused by Clint's courage. It retreated half a step. "You're a spineless fool. You're nothing." The words were empty and Clint knew it. Even more importantly, the beast knew that he knew it.

"Be quiet." The lion's mouth snapped shut as if it had been caught in an invisible vice. "Leave me now, or face the judgment of the King." Clint watched with disbelief as the massive head of the diabolos was dragged to the ground by some invisible millstone of submission. The thing scrambled backward, clawing the ground as if it were skating on ice. Then it flapped its reptilian wings, shot into the air, and it was gone.

"Sweet!" Clint could hardly believe it. "How did I ... we ... do that?" His heart was pounding as he looked around for the King. Force of habit.

"Authority trumps power in Basileia." The King could not be seen but was obviously still there. "Even though diabolon are greater than you and have supernatural strength, under my victory they are nothing.

"Clint, know this: Diabolon will tempt you to make these encounters about power. If you give in to that temptation, you can't win. But if you reject their bait, standing in my authority, you can't lose. And by the way, you're still seeing them like they want you to see them." Clint felt the King's invisible hands settle on his head. A vibrating sensation rippled through his skull.

"In the Old City people think that I'm at war with Pythus and his diabolon. But I have already defeated the dark ones. My war is over, or I could have no authority over them."

"But there is a war. I've seen it."

"Of course there is. With you. War is a contest of power, Clint. But with me there is no contest. Pythus knows that, so he's turned all his fury on the ones I love. On you. He wants to defeat my children. He wants to spite me for humiliating him at the battle of the bridge."

"You said that I don't have to fight him, but in the Old City I saw people seriously hurt and even killed in battle."

"Of course. Remember how the Book of Life becomes to you what you think it's for? If you treat the diabolon as foes to be fought, they will happily indulge you and you will have to endure many wounds and casualties. But if you deal with them as the defeated foes they are, they must submit to your authority. My authority in you."

"That's incredible."

"Yes. But behold your fearsome enemy."

The King suddenly reappeared, gripping a thick iron chain in his hand. At the end of the chain sat a gaunt old lion with tattered wings. The King reached out and grabbed one of its paws. There were no claws. Next he pried open the thing's mouth, and it complied without resistance. To Clint's astonishment, it had no teeth either. "I have disarmed your enemy," the King explained. The creature was obviously afraid of both Clint and the King, and would have taken flight if it hadn't been held in place by the King's hefty chain.

"Then what I saw earlier was a deception? An illusion?"

The King vanished again, along with the diabolos. "The dark ones are disarmed, but they still hold considerable power to deceive and intimidate. As you have experienced firsthand, they still have their roar. If you give in to fear, by that fear you will be devoured."

Clint nodded, then cocked his head to one side. "My sword." Clint scanned the ground for his weapon. "Sorry, I must have dropped it."

"You didn't drop it."

"Then where did it go?"

The King chuckled, and Clint's tongue tingled. "I put it in your mouth."

CHAPTER FOURTEEN:
CHANGE

"Clint, wake up."

Clint stirred, expecting to find the Shelah teasing at his bedside again. Or maybe his own daughter. Groping around in the pitch-blackness, he found that he was still in Vita's cottage.

Part of him was relieved. His friends had become like family to him. But part of him was disappointed. For a moment he thought he had been transported home again. Sadness washed over him momentarily, but he steeled himself against it. He had given that dream to the King.

Clint's eyes adjusted to the dim light. There was no one in the room with him. Not that he could see, anyway. But the King was there. "I'm awake. What's going on?"

"Come with me."

"Sure. Let me get dressed." Slipping out of bed, Clint shuffled his leaden feet toward his clothes. His toes began to tingle. A second later they lost contact with the floor.

He was flying.

With that, Clint spun around once and floated out the window, at peace with the shimmering air. He was being drawn toward the King. Giving himself up to the pull, he ascended higher and higher, rising until he hung like a graceful star two hundred feet above the city.

"Whoah, this is… wow."

A gentle breeze teased his skin, but he was strangely warm. It felt marvellous for his body to be weightless, much like his soul had felt the past few weeks. He could see the whole city from where he fluttered—Golgotha, the treasury, the shimmering streets, the temple, the home of his friends below. It was a truly magical moment.

"I've always wanted to fly."

"I love you too."

Something felt off. Slightly… odd. "This is a dream, isn't it?" The King nodded.

"Aw, nuts."

"But it's a real dream. From my heart to yours."

"Thank you." Clint sighed. Had it been a month since his nightmarish terrors at the spring of death?

"A month tomorrow. Do you like the New City?"

"I love it. I was made for this."

"Yes. And yet …"

"I still miss my family. My wife, my daughter, my home, my yard, my church family. Even my Highlander." He shrugged his shoulders. "I'm sorry. I will accept your will for me. I mean, I do."

"You're sorry? What for? You should miss them all. You were also created for them, Clint. Minus the Highlander."

The King laughed, then grew serious. "Things are going to change tomorrow."

"Change?"

"You need to trust me. In some ways, everything will seem different. But in truth, nothing will be."

"But what …"

"Clint, wake up!"

Bolting upright in a panic, Clint found Shelah really was at his bedside. Shaking his head, he tried to shed the cobwebs tangling up his brain. Facing her ever-present grin, he decided to tell her about his dream.

"I was flying."

"My dream was riding a horse in a field of clover and flowers."

"Your dream?"

"The one the King gave me before everything changed but nothing did."

"You … you had one too?"

"Yup. A long time ago. But the King asked me to wake you. Come on." He took her hand, then slid out of bed. Shelah led him through the house past Rosa and Vita—who looked concerned, though not overly worried. He wondered what was going on until she pushed open the screeching door. He gasped.

The shimmering air… was gone. The rippling pavement had vanished. The city's glow had faded.

Clint felt like he had put his finger into an electric socket. And his chest felt different. His head buzzed with shock. The spring was gone. The diabolon were gone, the darkness of Kakos was gone. Everything around him looked so normal and sickeningly plain. His stomach wrenched itself into a merciless knot.

"Clint… " Vita and Rosa had joined him outside.

His throat locked up, stuck on a sob too big to rise. "I can't, you guys. I can't go back. I hate that Old City. I can't live without the King. I can't."

"You don't have to," Vita said, reaching to embrace him.

"Don't be afraid," Rosa whispered.

"Don't be afraid? How can you say that? Over the past few weeks I've been given everything my soul has ever ached for and now it's gone. It's not fair. Why do you get to keep all your blessings?"

"We don't, sweetheart," Rosa said. "None of us do."

"What?"

"It's true." Clint saw the honesty radiating from Vita's eyes as usual. His heart sank like a stone.

"Then all of this wasn't real?"

"Oh, it was real. We all experienced the first few weeks of revelation like you did. But a day always comes when we have to walk by faith, not by sight."

"You mean none of you saw or heard all the things I saw the past few weeks?" He rubbed his jaw in disbelief.

"Not with our physical eyes and ears," Rosa explained. "But we experienced it in our hearts."

Clint didn't understand. How was it possible? Mercifully, they let him fumble through the weight of the moment. It felt like a bomb had been dropped on his faith.

"It's all here, Clint."

Clint gasped. The voice of the King, audible and rich and real. "What's happening to me? What's going on?"

"I'm taking you home, one step at a time." This time the voice was in his mind.

"Home? I thought I wasn't going home."

"I never said that. I just wanted you to be at home here before sending you back. Now you can draw the realities of Basileia into your old life."

"My old life? In the Old City?"

"That wasn't life, Clint. I mean your old life with your family, your job, your yard, and even your Highlander. By the way, your lawn needs mowing."

Next, Basileia itself started fading from view. Clint felt a wave of profound sadness. And then, a quivering, childlike excitement took it's place. He wanted to stay with the King, to live in Basileia. The truth was, he wasn't sure he could ever feel at home in the earthly realm now, but the thought of seeing Monica and Sarah made his chest pound with anticipation. The knot in his gut began to loosen.

A moment later the medieval city was gone. It had been replaced by his house, his yard, and his driveway. He was standing like a stranger in his old neighbourhood.

Looking beyond his yard, Clint's heart skipped like a stone bounding across a little pond. Vita, Rosa, and Shelah were standing on a porch just four houses down, arms folded across their chests, grinning from ear to ear, as if they had been waiting for this moment.

"What? Is this possible?"

"We're here, aren't we?"

Clint charged like a teenage bull across all four yards, leaping over planters and dodging parked vehicles, not stopping until he had nearly tackled his old friends and wrapped his arms around all of them in a giant bear hug.

"What are you doing here? And your clothes. Look at you. You're not peasants anymore."

"We live here, silly." Shelah poked his ribs, giggling.

"What?"

Vita and Rosa were beaming. "We're those neighbours you never quite had the nerve to come and meet," Rosa said, scolding playfully.

"I know Sarah from school," Shelah said, piping in. "We've both got Miss Preeble for Math."

"I found you curled up in the fetal position on your front steps the other day," Vita explained. "It wasn't pretty. You've been staying with us since then, with Monica gone for the weekend and all."

"But I thought you lived in Basileia!"

"We do, Clint. Don't you remember what the King said?"

"I said that my kingdom overlaps your world." It was the King's voice sounding inside him.

"You mean ..."

"He means that the New City, the grace, the air, the spring, the cross, the treasury, all of it, is right here, waiting for you to embrace in this world. Your faith in the King brings them all home."

Home. The word meant so much more than it had a month ago.

"The diabolon and Kakos and the chasm and the bridge are here too." Shelah nodded vigorously, obviously pleased with her wisdom.

"My Father and I never stop working to manifest the realities of Basileia on earth, in this realm," the King said. "In Basileia my desires are always reality, but on earth they conflict with the wills of a million others. In those glorious moments when my desires are welcomed from Basileia to earth through the faith of your heart, miracles happen. The dead are raised. The lame are healed. Lives change. The prisoners are set free. Basileia is built. My kingdom pours into this realm."

Clint's head was spinning. "Oh boy. I think I'm gonna need more faith."

"No, you don't," Shelah said, correcting him.

"She's right. A mustard seed's worth of faith is all I need from you," said the King.

Clint gasped. It was true. He could suddenly feel it. Or not exactly feel.

It was deeper than that. A profound knowing from the core of his being. Every lesson he had learned, every moment of the whole adventure—even in the Old City—had prepared him for his normal life here on earth. He was going to say "in the real world," but he realized that Basileia was the real world too. He almost said "at home," but Basileia had become home too—as normal and real as the buckling cement on his driveway. They were both real and home at the same time.

The saying was true: Home really was where the heart is, and his heart was in both places. That was the lesson he had been given.

The next moment nearly knocked him over. Clint's brain finally caught up with his faith, and it all came back to him—in his mind's eye, that is. He could feel the spring within him. He knew the King's presence. He heard his voice in his heart. He saw the shimmering, glorious air of the kingdom. He felt the grace beneath his feet and the riches of the King's treasury. It was all here, all real, all the time. Though his eyes couldn't see it, he knew it. And that knowing was more powerful than any feeling. Stronger than anything else on earth.

Vita put his hand on Clint's shoulder. "Sometimes the King peels back the veil and gives us glimpses of the New City. But mostly, he just helps us remember the truth and live it out. The hard part is living with a foot in each realm, which means facing the constant tension between what we see by faith and what we see with our eyes."

"And doing that without losing heart," Rosa said, completing his thought.

"Yup. And one day we'll go live with him in Basileia forever." Shelah's eyes sparkled like her daddy's.

"Faith will become sight," the King said. "I can hardly wait for that day, Clint. I'm already preparing a special place for you in my New City."

Clint nodded, rubbing his eyes as if trying to wake up. "You know, I think I'm going to be okay." He would have kept blabbering but his reverie was interrupted by a silver Highlander gliding down the street.

HonkHonk!

It was Monica and Sarah. The girls had stepped out for the weekend to give him some space. The weekend? His whole adventure had taken just a few days?

"Time is my plaything," the King said.

Clint laughed. "Works for me." He eyed the van as it pulled into the driveway. "May I?"

"What are you waiting for?"

Clint bounded over to the van and nearly ripped the sliding door off its hinges. "Monica, honey, I met the King. I really did. I went to live in Basileia and I'm back now, and wow, do I have a story to tell you."

Monica looked at him blankly. "Basileia?"

"The kingdom of God. Give or take. It was so cool."

"And you ... you ... went there?"

Clint nodded, stilled by the solemnity of the moment. "I'm still there now. All three of us are, actually." He knew how foolish it all sounded, but he didn't care. It was the truth. His new reality.

"Right here? On the driveway?"

"Uh huh. Isn't it great?" He stomped his feet in excitement. Monica tilted her head heavenward and began to laugh. Sarah leaned forward, trying to wiggle out of her Highlander seat.

"What's so funny, Mommy? Daddy, why is Mommy laughing at you?"

They ignored her for the time being. "Really, Clint? Basileia?"

Clint nodded. "I know how it sounds, hon…"

But tears had already spilled over her eyelids, marking her cheeks with a ragged joy. Resting her forehead on the steering wheel, she whispered a heartfelt prayer.

"Thank you, King. Thank you."

— —-

The End

EPIL⊕GUE

It's time to lower the curtain on Basileia, leaving joyful Clint (me) bear-hugging his family on the driveway.

Where does that leave you? Maybe you resonate with the kingdom picture I've been painting. Maybe you're already living that kind of life. But maybe not. Maybe you're still wrestling with the concepts. Either way, I'm pretty sure I've made you think, and that's beautiful.

Personally speaking, I'm done living in the Old City—along with its soul-killing striving, seeking, thirsting, and fighting— praise God. I'm absolutely convinced that King Jesus opened up a new and living way for me through his death and resurrection. I'm increasingly experiencing that dynamic way of life—a path marked by loving, trusting, enjoying, and reigning.

Along with that, I'm learning to live with one foot in this world and another in Christ's kingdom—my true country—the eternal realm pulsing just beyond the veil of my senses. As you can tell, I'm never going back. I hope you come along for the ride if you haven't already.

I hope you've seen the truth that your perspective determines your experience. I hope I've evoked something, that I've poked something and awakened fresh faith in your soul. I pray that your heart is having a personal apocalypse—a revelation of Christ that changes life as you know it.

I've just lobbed the proverbial ball into your court. Now it's your turn. You've got to write yourself into the story and finish the tale in real life.

I'm guessing that at least some of you are asking good questions: "What about angels, or the routines of work or family or school? What about (fill in the blank)?" And I get that. I know perfectly well that I haven't told the whole story or written a fully orbed manifesto of the Christian life. It's a parable, and parables aren't supposed to nail everything down. We're trying to get away from "the old way of the written code," remember? My advice is to let *Realms* be what it is. It's only a parable, right?

Or is it?

Remember the toothless greeter at the city gate? His question still stands.

Old City or New City?